After
All
These
Years

My life
as a Christian

by

Stephen Sweetman

Contents

Disclaimer..6

Dedication...7

Now That I'm Sixty Eight 8

Defining Christian.................................11

1 - Visually Impaired.............................13

2 - Healed Of Juvenile Diabetes............22

3 - Altar Calls...32

4 - Billy Graham....................................38

5 - The Next Day...................................43

6 - The Holy Spirit................................. 46

7 - Redefining My Experience...................56

8 - Spiritually Schizophrenic.................... 61

9 - The Jesus People Movement...............65

10 - Demons 71

11 - Elim Bible Institute And College.......76

12 - The Shepherding Movement..............80

13 - Moving To Virginia...........................83

14 - Politics..88

15 - A New Home.....................................93

16 - Another Son.......................................99

17 - Our Church Closes............................101

18 - Divorce..104

19 - Get Lost...108

20 - I'm From Eastern Canada..................112

21- Good-bye Bill..................................120

22 - Figuring Out Church..........................123

23 - Home Bible Study............................. 126

24 - www.stevesweetman.com................. 133

25 - Ordained To Ministry.......................138

26 - Cancer... 144

27 - December 4, 2019 147

28 - After All These Years.......................150

29 - The Process Of Salvation...................154

About The Author 160

All Scripture quotations, unless otherwise indicated, are taken from the Holy Bible, New International Version®, NIV®. Copyright ©1973, 1978, 1984, 2011 by Biblica, Inc.™ Used by permission of Zondervan. All rights reserved worldwide.

www.zondervan.com The "NIV" and "New International Version" are trademarks registered in the United States Patent and Trademark Office by Biblica, Inc.™

Disclaimer

This book has not been edited by someone else as is usually the case with my books. Therefore, because of me being legally blind, and, not being a professional editor, you may find some errors in what you read. Hopefully you will not find many mistakes. If you do come across some, just contact me and I will correct them. Corrections are relatively easy with these Amazon books.

My contact information can be found at the end of the book.

Dedication

I dedicate this book to my wife Dianne. If by chance I pass into the next life before her, she can refresh her memory of my life with Jesus as she reads my testimony in this book. I also dedicate this project to my two sons, Jeremy Lee and Jonathan Robert. After I depart from this life, they too will have something to read about their father and his life as a Christian. Then, beyond my immediate family, I dedicate this book to my extended family members. I want everyone to know that I have lived my life for the Lord Jesus Christ. My hope is that all who read this brief account of my life will do the same.

Now That I'm Sixty Eight

In 1967 the Beatles released one of their most popular and best selling record albums. It was long before the days of CD's, and even long before the days of cassette tapes. This album was a watershed album in the Beatles career because it presented its fans with a different and definite change in the style of their music and recordings from that point on. It was released in 1967 when what was then called "psychedelic music" blasted its way onto the hippie influenced, musical cultural scene. The album's title was called "Sgt. Pepper's Lonely Hearts Club Band." I have that album on compact disc.

One of the sound tracks from that album was a song entitled "When I'm Sixty Four." Being sixty four years old probably seemed a very long way off into the future for the "fab four," as they were often called. In case you don't know, the word "fab" is short form for fabulous. The Beatles were the most popular singing group in the world in the 1960's. According to most, especially their female fans, they were simply fabulous.

As I write these words in the autumn of 2019, the two surviving Beatles, Paul McCartney and Ringo Starr, have surpassed the age of sixty four, something they must really shake their heads at, as most senior citizens do when they officially become seniors at the age of sixty five. Both McCartney and Starr are now half way through their seventies.

Like Paul McCartney and Ringo Starr, I too, have surpassed my sixty fourth birthday. Now that I'm almost sixty eight years old, I'd like to share with you part of the story of my life as a Christian. Being a Christian is fundamental to whom I have been, and still am, and forever will be.

So, sit back. Pour yourself a cup of tea, coffee, or a glass of wine. If you prefer a beer, go ahead. That is certainly fine with me. This is not a long read. My hope and prayer is that my story will be both informative and inspiring. I've lived a pretty simple, and really, not an overly exciting life. So you ask: "Why write a book about a non-eventful life?" Well, the answer is not difficult to figure out. I'm writing this book because I want to. I want to tell you about my life as a Christian. I'd like to leave some kind of legacy once I depart from this life. Maybe my ordinary story will be a blessing to other ordinary people like me, and that's probably you. If you think about it for a moment, most all of us are just ordinary people. Besides that, I may be quite ordinary, but Jesus, the Son of the Almighty, Creator, God, is far from ordinary. He lives within me by His Spirit. You might then call me, at least in a spiritual sense, extra-ordinary.

God bless you as you read on.

Defining Christian

I am a Christian as defined in conservative, New Testament, Biblical terms.

A Christian is one, whom by the assistance of God's Holy Spirit, has chosen to stop serving his own selfish, sinful, nature. With the help of the Spirit of God he has decided to enter into a trusting relationship with the Lord Jesus Christ. The validating proof of one being a genuine Christian is that he will exhibit the reality of God's Holy Spirit living within him. There will be noticeable evidence of him being a true Christian in his life.

The apostle Paul, in 2 Corinthians 5:17 explained being a genuine Christian this way. He said:

> "Therefore, if anyone is in Christ, the new creation has come: The old has gone, the new is here!"

I like how the older version of the New International Bible puts 2 Corinthians 5:17. It says that a Christian is one who is "a new creation." A Christian, then, is someone who he once was not. He is in fact, a brand new Creation, and he is so, because of the Holy Spirit living within him. It only makes sense, that if the Creator God, by His Spirit, lives within one, that one is a new creation. For this reason, I often say this. "As a woman is different from a man, so a Christian is different from a non-Christian."

Me, at a very young age.

1
Visually Impaired

I don't recall my mother giving birth to me, but this I know. According to what I have been told, and my birth certificate proves it to be true; I was born in Belleville, Ontario, Canada, on December 4th, 1951. Don't ask me when I was conceived. I don't seem to recall that either. Apparently, no one has ever felt that bit of information was important enough to pass onto me.

My birth would certainly have been quite an event to remember. I can only begin to imagine my birth experience after I watched my two sons, Jeremy Lee and Jonathan Robert, being born into this world, and they were two very amazing, even incredible, experiences.

My mother (Beatrice Reba, born April 12, 1921 - died January 9 2003) was a Christian when she birthed me onto this planet. My father, however, was not a Christian when I made my entrance into this life. Why my mother, as a Christian, married a non-Christian, is unknown to me as well, but she did. Whatever the case, Jesus did turn my dad around a few years after I was born. Jesus is quite capable of turning around people's lives.

My father (Clifford Gerald, born on July 18, 1923 - died June 7, 2001) was a railroader, as they used to call people like dad. He worked for the Canadian National Railroad for close to fifty years, as did his father (Charles Henry, born August 20, 1887 - died March, 1984). Dad played steel guitar in a popular local country music band in the late 1940's. His band had their own weekly radio show on our local radio station, CJBQ. The band would also play their music and songs at various dances throughout the greater Belleville region.

Within the first two years of my life there appeared to be something seriously wrong with my eyes. I had to get extremely close to everything I did in order to see things properly, as I am doing right now, as I reread these words.

My first recollection in life was when my mother dropped a penny onto the carpeted, living-room, floor. I was about two years old at the time when mom asked me to pick the penny up from the floor for her. I struggled to do so since the colour of the penny and the colour of the carpet were very similar. There was not sufficient contrast between the penny and the carpet for me to see the penny properly. The penny blended into the carpet. As a result of my hesitation, mom became a bit agitated with me. I did not pick up the penny as promptly as she wanted. Her agitation is probably why I remember the incident so vividly. Mom thought I was ignoring her request, or simply fooling around. I was doing neither. I just could not see the penny.

Around the age of three, one of my Sunday-school teachers told my mother that her and dad should take me to see an eye doctor. In her exact words she said this: "I don't think Stevie sees very well." She was correct about that. Stevie did not see well at all.

The eye doctor confirmed that I had very bad eyesight. As a matter of fact, I was, and still am, legally blind. The doctor told my parents that I had roughly four percent vision in both eyes, especially when it came to seeing fine details. Less than ten percent vision in both eyes, with the assistance of corrective lenses, is considered to be legally blind in Canada.

Years ago I tested my son Jonathan's eyesight. He could see to read a one inch letter from twenty eight feet away. For me to read the same one inch letter I need to be about two inches from the letter.

My poor eye sight has had a profound effect on my life over the years, as you might expect. As I read these words that I have typed on my computer, my nose is almost scraping my twenty-seven inch monitor, even with the assistance of large print software that makes the letters almost one inch tall on the screen.

My nose often gets black with ink as it scrapes its way across the printed page when I attempt to read. So, if you ever see me with a black, ink-stained, nose, please know that I am not a racist. I'm not trying to be black. I've just forgotten to clean the ink stain off the tip of my nose.

Attending school, through the normal, public, school system, was not easy for me. Trying to figure out and understand, and get into my brain, words and sentences on a black board that I could not see to read was a difficulty I was forced to work through.

In order for me to even attempt to read what was written on the black board, I would often shove my desk close to the black board. On one occasion a substitute teacher who did not know me came into the room to relieve our regular teacher. He noticed me sitting a foot away from the black board and asked why I was sitting there. I responded by saying that I could not see well. He did not believe me. He thought I was being punished for some wrong doing. He, then, pretended he was blind by bumping into things and feeling his way around the black board with his hands. The class broke out in hysteric laughter. What was funny to my classmates was extremely embarrassing for me as a ten year old, somewhat shy, boy. Come that evening, that teacher received a very stern phone call from my very upset father.

It was suggested to my mom and dad early on in my life that they send me to a school for visually impaired and blind children that was about three hours away from our home town. One of the biggest favours my parents ever did for me was to not send me to that school. By attending a regular school I was forced to live in the real world with my disability, instead of living in the protected world of a school for the blind.

I have noticed that with many visually impaired and blind people, their blindness is not their major disability. Their major disability is being unable to fit into a sighted society. They come across as being culturally awkward because they were raised in a protected and secluded environment. That was not me as a child, and is not me to this very day. I have always wanted to fit in with the rest of the general public, and anyone who knows me, knows that I have succeeded in that.

Finding gainful employment as an adult was also not easy for me. It was something that I never really did accomplish in my life. I'm not really happy about that fact. I did work in some jobs, but all of my attempts to find a long-lasting, satisfying, career ended in failure. That does not do a lot for one's self-confidence and self-esteem, especially when you are a man. Men are often judged by what they do, and not by who they are. Nevertheless, no matter what man thinks of me, I know how God thinks of me, and that is what really counts in my life. I have learned that true self-esteem and self-confidence comes from knowing who I am, and that is, a Christian who has trusted Jesus with his life.

If we are ever to find any sense of worth, value, or security in who we are, we can only find it when we receive it from the One who is the most worthy, most valuable, and most secure in Himself. That is the Lord Jesus Christ.

Beyond finding value in the Lord, Jesus has rescued me on two major occasions from being killed, or at least, injured bodily for life. On one occasion I was crossing a four lane street here in town. I know what you are thinking. Why, were you, a legally blind guy, and an adult at that, trying to cross a four lane street? Okay, I concede. You have a valid point to make. It might well have been a stupid thing to do, but really, I was sure I heard no cars coming down that street. Hearing no cars while crossing streets is important for me. I cross a street more by listening for cars than trying to see cars I cannot see very well, if at all. If I don't listen, I can't cross. So, because I did not hear any cars, I crossed that four lane street. Actually, I got half way cross, and then it happened.

As I was saying, I heard no cars on the street. This unheard car must have come flying from a side street, and flying is the appropriate word. He was travelling way too fast for this city street. No wonder I did not hear him, that is, until it was almost too late. As I heard the squeal of his braking tires, my first reaction was to run in the hope of escaping a serious collision, but I could not run. It was as if Jesus, or and angel from Heaven, prevented my feet from moving. When the car came to a stop, it was one foot away from me. I came that close to death. If I had taken one step farther, I doubt if I would be here today to type these words.

On another occasion I was just about to cross a two lane street, when a quiet voice from within said: "Don't cross." I did not cross the street, and I am glad. Within one second after haring that inner voice, a car came zooming by, and again, way too fast for that residential street.

I relate these things to you to say this. Despite the fact that Jesus has not healed my eyes, His hand of protection is always on my life. He always provides for me. For example, when I entered grade 9, when print in the text books was way too small for me to read, my mom and dad discovered the glasses I read with today. My first pair of reading glasses were purchased from an eye doctor in Buffalo, New York, whom dad took me to see. These glasses have a magnifier in the right lens. I thus read, by scraping my nose across the printed page, while reading out of my right eye. Without these glasses I would not have graduated from high school.

Even though Jesus has not healed my eyes, He has beyond any doubt, compensated for this lack of healing. That's the way it is, for me a Christian.

Mom loved my curly hair. I have
learn to put up with it. She saved some of my
curls in a glass jar, which I still have.

2
Healed Of Juvenile Diabetes

There was another problem in my young life that manifested itself around the age of five years. I remember taking five or six cookies to bed with me each night and drinking tons of water throughout the day. Okay, tons of water is a bit of an exaggeration. I drank many, too many, cups of water each day. Does that sound better?

All of those cookies and cups of water got my parents quite concerned. To make one of many long stories short that you will read in this book, I ended up at Sick Children's Hospital, in Toronto, Ontario, Canada. There, the doctors diagnosed me having Juvenile Diabetes, a pretty severe, even deadly, illness for a little boy.

I vividly recall those days. I remember going to Toronto on the train with dad, taking a taxi to Sick Children's Hospital, and, looking out my hospital-room window from many floors above the street below. I recall the hospital's playroom, but most of all, I recall getting my finger pricked for blood and drinking glucose, that sickening sweet tasting stuff that flipped my stomach in all directions. I'll never forget that horrible taste. How can something that tastes so sweet become so sickening once in your stomach? According to Revelation 10:10, that is quite possible.

> "I took the little scroll from the angel's hand and ate it. It tasted as sweet as honey in my mouth, but when I had eaten it, my stomach turned sour."

During those days my mother was part of a new church in our town that met in the basement of a home on the corner of Symington Drive and Herchimer Avenue, in east-end Belleville. It was the beginning days of the Free Methodist Church in our town in the early 1950's.

With news of my illness, the pastor, Edith Mainprize, and others decided to have special prayer for me on one predetermined Sunday morning. When that Sunday was approaching, my mom forewarned dad, in no uncertain terms, that he had to be at that Sunday church meeting. Dad was not in the habit of attending church meetings back then, but this one was special, so mom made sure dad was there. "We will pray for Stevie," she told dad. "You must be there."

Miss Mainprize anointed me with oil in compliance with James 5:14. That verse reads:

> "Is anyone among you sick? Let them call the elders of the church to pray over them and anoint them with oil in the name of the Lord."

At that point, Miss Mainprize and a few others laid their hands on me and prayed that God's will would be done in my life. I clearly recall that day and that moment. The little homemade platform with an altar rail around three sides of the platform was situated at one end of the basement room. I knelt in prayer on the right side of the platform while people prayed for me.

For the record, in these days when so many Christians claim or even demand healing from God because, as some say, we are the King's kids; there was no such prayer prayed that morning. The prayer, as old fashion as it may sound to some today, was simply this. "May your will be done, Lord Jesus."

On that precise day, Jesus performed a miracle in my life. That very Sunday afternoon my mom told my dad that Jesus had healed me of Diabetes. She believed that to be the case because I did not drink any water that entire afternoon, and that was not normal for me. Dad, being quite skeptical, replied by saying that if Jesus really did heal me, the doctors at Sick Children's Hospital would confirm that, so via a train, off to Toronto we went.

The doctors did confirm that a miracle had transpired in my life. There words were simple and direct. "There is not a trace of Diabetes in your son's body," they told dad in confirmation of the miracle. Although the doctors did admit to a miracle, they could not bring themselves to attribute the miracle to Jesus, but dad knew the truth about that. It did not take long for dad to hand his life over to Jesus after knowing for sure that Jesus had delivered me from this devastating sickness.

For some reason, which is beyond my understanding, Jesus did not heal my eye problem when he healed me of Juvenile

Diabetes. Of course, there is no doubt that He could have healed my legally blind eyes. I have no doubt about that. He just chose not to. I'm sure He had His reasons. Whatever the case, He hasn't healed me yet, but if it is His will, He certainly can and certainly will heal me. One thing I know for sure, and that is this. When I pass from this life, and, when I receive my eternal body in the next life, I will be healed. Thank you Jesus.

At times I think that my life could have been far more productive for the Lord if I could have had good eyesight over the years, but what was, is what was. I can't do anything about that now. I can only serve Jesus to the best of my ability right now, in present time. Healing people of illnesses is God's decision, not mine, and not yours.

The exact problem with my eyes is that most all of the nerve endings that connect my eyes to my brain are dead. Don't misread what I've just wrote. It's not my brain that is dead. It's the thousands of nerve endings behind my eyes that are dead. I just wanted to clarify that one. I was born with these dead nerve cells.

One eye doctor in Toronto told me that in all of his ten thousand patients; only four others have eye problems like mine. My father had the same eye problem but not to the same extent. He could drive a car. There is no way that I can drive a car, and if I did attempt to drive, you would surely be walking and not sitting in the passenger seat.

I view my non-healing, at least to date, this way. Do you remember the three Hebrew men that were thrown into the furnace of fire that you read about in the book of Daniel? In Daniel 3:17 and 18 they said that they believed God could deliver them from the flames of fire, but even if He did not rescue them, they would still trust Him and not bow to the King's idol. In my thinking, those men exhibited true Biblical faith, true trust in God. Those men would continue to trust in God even if God did not do as they asked or hoped for. It's the same for me. That is how I view my non-healing.

Here is what Daniel 3:17 and 18 say.

> "If we are thrown into the blazing furnace, the God we serve is able to deliver us from it, and he will deliver us from Your Majesty's hand. But even if he does not, we want you to know, Your Majesty,

that we will not serve your gods or worship the image of gold you have set up."

Don't let the words "but even if He does not ..." mislead you. Those words do not suggest doubt, or lack of faith, as many think. They express ultimate trust in God; a trust that stays strong when God appears to be silent.

Some hyper-faith folk have told me that I have a lack of faith, and that lack of faith prevents me from being healed of my legally blind eyes. I do not believe that for a second. Like those three Jewish men in the Old Testament book of Daniel, I trust my entire life with Jesus, whether He heals my legally blind eyes or not. To me that is true faith. That's faith that stands firm until the end, whether the end is bitter or glorious.

Faith is not trying to convince yourself in a humanistic way that God can do anything for you. Faith is not trying to trick your mind into believing you have received something from God when in fact you have not. Faith is not a commodity that you can get more of. Faith, as defined in the Bible, and is understood by the Greek word "pistis" that is translated as faith and believe in the English New Testament, means trust. Faith is simply trusting Jesus.

Faith is resting in the fact that you can trust your life with Jesus, no matter what happens, whether it's good, bad, or indifferent.

One of my Sunday-school teachers was my grade eight teacher. He told my dad after I graduated from his grade eight class that he always thought the teachers in earlier grades were just passing me along to the next grade, even though I did not actually pass the grade. After I graduated from his class, he told my dad that he had changed his mind. He said that I worked hard, and, that I passed all of my tests. He did not pass me onto the next grade out of pity for me.

I believe Martin Luther (one of the fathers of the Christian Reformation - born November 10, 1483 - died February 18, 1546) was Biblically correct when he said that faith is a passive action, and, that passive action of faith produces active and productive works. You might want to think about that statement. If you embrace it, I believe it will change the way you think about your faith. It might even change your life.

Since the time of my healing of Juvenile Diabetes and my father's conversion to Jesus, throughout my growing up years my dad would take his guitar here, there, and everywhere. He would play Christian music with his brothers in Christ. You could find him at camp meetings and in church services across southern Ontario. In those meetings, dad would never fail to tell the story of my healing. That was his mission. Being centered out like that became embarrassing for me, but that didn't stop dad from telling everybody that Jesus had healed me. That was just the way it was. I got used to being embarrassed.

The story of my healing was spoken one last time at the side of my father's death bed. I told the story to dad's neighbour who came to visit my dying father in the hospital. Dad could no longer tell his story of my healing for himself, so on behalf of dad, I told his story. My father was just too far gone to say a word, let alone tell his story. Cancer would kill him in a matter of a few minutes. I told dad's neighbour how Jesus had healed me of Juvenile Diabetes as a child. I told the man how dad, because of my healing, gave his life to Jesus.

While I told my father's story for him, my wife Dianne noticed one lonely tear slide down dad's cheek. I knew dad could hear what I had said. My words, really his testimony, must have penetrated his heart.

I, then, laid my hands on my father. I asked Jesus to take him, and He did. Ten minutes later, and two minutes after we left my father's room, he died. My dad was, in the good sense of the word, a proud man. He would do anything for you. He just found it difficult to have others do for him as he did for them. I am convinced that my father did not want to die in anyone's presence, not even in the presence of one of his children. For this reason he chose to die once he knew we were on our way home. What a glorious way to leave this life.

Assisting my dad to relocate to heaven, as I believe my wife Dianne and I did through our prayer, was an awesome experience. I seldom speak the word "awesome," but that was awesome. I reserve that word for Jesus, but asking Jesus to take my dad at that exact moment, was beyond any doubt, an awesome Jesus experience.

3
Altar Calls

While being raised in an Evangelical church environment in the 1950's and 1960's you had ample opportunities to commit your life to the Lord Jesus and get saved. These opportunities were called altar calls. Even though the congregation consisted of Christians, every Sunday morning and evening we were all given the chance to walk forward to the altar and get saved, even if we got saved last Sunday. So that is what I did. That is, I got saved every other Sunday or so. It was usually an emotional experience of prayer that made me feel good at the time, but come the next day, well, I woke feeling like the same old me.

Where was that glorious, heavenly, feeling I had experienced the evening before? Did I lose it during my night's sleep? Did I really get saved? Did I commit some kind of sin on the way home from church that unsaved me? Did I have a bad dream that kicked the good feelings out of me? Did the devil somehow sneak into my bedroom and rob me of my salvation? Maybe I really didn't get saved the evening before and that is why I felt unsaved Monday morning. Can one actually get unsaved? Is the word "unsaved" a real word, or is it an invention of poor lost Evangelical young souls like myself?

With all of those trips to the altar to find salvation, nothing really seemed to change in my life. The feelings from the evening before were long gone the next day and I had no clue where they went, or, if they would ever return again.

It was my routine each evening at bed time to say a short little prayer and read a couple of Bible verses from a very large print gospel of John. As my nose slid across the page of that gospel of John, it just seemed to be the right thing to do. It was just enough religiosity to appease the ever-present feelings of guilt. I now realize that guilt is not a feeling. That I did not know back then. Guilt is the position in which we stand before the Lord. Whether we feel guilty or not, without Jesus' forgiveness, we are guilty. Although guilty feelings are certainly a distraction and hindrance to your life as a Christian, they mean nothing when it comes to your standing before God and your salvation.

Some of these feelings associated with guilt were a result of my lack of understanding of Scripture. They were also prevalent in my life because of the teaching I heard in Sunday school and in Sunday sermons. I remember one Sunday-school teacher scaring us with this idea. If we ever told a little white lie as we used to call it, and, if we neglected or forgot to ask to be forgiven; we'd end up in the Lake of Fire, commonly, but mistakenly, known as hell. As a side note, and Biblically speaking, hell is not the Lake of Fire. Hell is Hades, the present place of the unbelieving dead.

I was always truthful but I knew I was not perfect, so how would I ever make Heaven under those conditions? I never knew if I was in or out when it came to Heaven and hell. It seemed that I would get to the gate of Heaven, and just as I was about to step inside, I'd trip and slip back into the burning flames of hell. How disappointing and discouraging that felt. Of course, for me, it was all about feelings. Again, I now understand that feelings are irrelevant when it comes to my standing before God and my salvation.

Back and forth I went. Up front to the altar and back home to the usual routine of trying to rid myself of feelings associated with guilt. Usually, a short prayer and a few Bible verses normally did the trick, so to speak. That would make me a good Evangelical young person, or so I thought. It might just secure my place in Heaven some day. I certainly did not want to die in my sleep as the pastor told us was a good possibility. Who knows where I would end up then. At least the reading of a couple of verses and a short prayer relieved by guilty feelings for a few minutes. I could fall asleep with some kind, even a bit, of hope of not burning in the eternal and torrential flames of unquenchable fire.

You see, our church preached that we were saved by faith in God's grace. I certainly have no problem with that. That is good theology. Look at what Ephesians 2:8 says about being saved by faith in God's grace.

> "For it is by grace you have been saved, through faith — and this is not from yourselves, it is the gift of God —"

I knew that salvation was a matter of faith in God's grace, but, it appeared to me that staying saved was a matter of doing all sorts of good things and not doing all sorts of bad things. That included little, insignificant, bad things that most take for granted. That's not really what Romans 1:17 says. Read it for yourself.

> "For in the gospel the righteousness of God is revealed — a righteousness that is by faith from first to last, just as it is written: 'The righteous will live by faith.'"

Staying saved, like getting saved, is a matter of faith. It's about trusting, not just your salvation with Jesus, but your whole life with Him. The righteous will live by faith, according to Romans 1:17. Those people whom God considers to be righteous will live each day by trusting their lives to the Lord Jesus Christ.

Even though I made countless trips to the altar, there was one such trip that stands out among the rest. All of these trips are blurred into one foggy mess at this moment in time, but this one is not a part of the fog. I was about eleven years old when I dedicated my life to Jesus at an altar of prayer in the Free Methodist Church, on Avondale Road, in Belleville, Ontario, Canada. This response to the altar was different than others. It was not about finding forgiveness of sins. It was about dedicating my life to Jesus. It was about me, handing my life over to Jesus so He could use me in His service, but still, that did not end my confusion over whether I was forgiven of my sins or not. Those guilty feelings still plagued me until February, 1970, when that all changed for good.

4
Billy Graham

Most Saturday evenings at eight o'clock, were reserved to watch Hockey Night in Canada on television. That was the custom for many Canadians back in the 1950's and 1960's, and still is for many Canadians today. I would turn our television to the Canadian Broadcasting Corporation (CBC) and sit back and watch the game of the week. Actually, I could not sit back. I had to sit up, close to the TV to see what I was watching. Watching television is not necessarily a relaxing thing for me. I can't sit back on the couch and enjoy the program. The older I get, the harder it is to find a position in front of the television that does not hurt my aching back.

By the way, there were only six teams in the National Hockey League in the long-forgotten world of the 1950's and 1960's, even though what I am about to describe took place in 1970. I guess things do change over the years.

My favourite hockey team was the Chicago Black Hawks. That was due to the fact that hockey's best player, Bobby Hull, was our home-town hero.

I watched Hockey Night in Canada on channel eleven. On one particular Saturday evening in February, 1970, our television just happened to be turned to channel eight. We did not have remote controls back in those days so I could not just key in channel eleven on a remote control, and bingo, it would suddenly, next to miraculously, appear on the TV screen. As difficult as it may sound today, people had to go to the television, manually turn a knob on the TV, and work their way up from channel eight to channel eleven, the slow, old fashion, way. I realize that may be difficult for some to imagine these days, in our twenty-first century, high-tech and hand-held device, culture, but that was our low-tech reality back then. To my distress, I noticed that Billy Graham was preaching away on channel ten. I was trapped in the proverbial pickle, as they used to say way back when. Just who "they" are, is unknown to me.

I wanted to watch hockey on channel eleven but my weak Evangelical Christian conscience would not permit me to pass by Billy Graham. How in the name of heaven could a good Christian young person skip over Billy

Graham just to watch a hockey game that had no eternal value? It did not set right in my youthful, guilt-ridden, conscience. Passing Billy Graham by in the hope of watching Bobby Hull, well, that was next to the unforgivable sin, and what was that unforgivable sin anyway? That was always a big question among us church youth.

I figured that the unforgivable sin had something to do with sex, because the topic of sex was the unspeakable topic of discussion back then, that, despite the fact that sex was a natural and biological phenomenon that was exploding within our teenage bodies. The only thing I recall hearing about sex was this. "Take a cold shower and it will all go away," but it didn't go away. The urge always came back. One thing I know is that if I took all the cold showers I was encouraged to take, I'd be one very clean guy.

If I did not stay on channel ten and watch Billy Graham, at least for a few minutes, my Biblically illiterate conscience would tell me that I would be condemn for the rest of the day, and who knows, maybe even the rest of my life. I couldn't take any chance on being eternally condemned. To avoid that, I stayed on channel ten and listened to Billy Graham, not just for a few minutes, but for the entire hour.

I watched all of Billy Graham that evening. Yes, I sat and watched it all, right to the closing altar call. O no! Here was yet another altar call. What was I about to do with yet another altar call, especially when I could not walk up to the altar that I saw on television?

Billy Graham preached on Christians being lukewarm when in fact they were to be either hot or cold. He told us that the Lord was not all that happy with lukewarm Christians as could be seen in Revelation 3:15 and 16, and that was me. It was sad to admit, but I was a lukewarn believer, and that, in the vernacular of our day, scared the hell out of me. Literally, it really did.

After watching the program I went straight to bed, and as usual, I prayed. What else could I do? That was my usual routine, but this time, Billy Graham's preaching, or maybe it was the Holy Spirit, gave me more motivation to pray.

I only prayed for a short three to five seconds. That was it. It was not a long, drawn-out, emotional, prayer. When the Spirit of God is at work within a person, things don't always have to take forever. This prayer was definitely different than all of my other evening prayers. In a bit of frustrated concern for my sad soul, I simply prayed this: "Lord Jesus, if I am not forgiven, please (emphasis on the word "please") forgive me now." Word for word, that was the prayer. There was no emotion; no altar call, no pleading preacher, and no singing all seven verses of the old hymn "Just As I Am" four or five times over, as was sometimes the case in Evangelical church circles back then. It was just a matter of fact prayer that changed my life for good.

Me, in 1968 while in grade 11.

5
The Nest Day

The next day, which was in mid February, 1970, was different for me. Unlike all of the emotional times spent at an altar of prayer, this unemotional short request of a prayer the evening before managed to do something in my life all of the altar calls did not do. Maybe I should say it this way. Jesus did something in my life that did not leave me thinking I got unsaved over night. That morning I woke wanting to read my Bible. I wanted to pray. I wanted to do the things Jesus desires Christians to do. I wanted to be that hot Christian Billy Graham preached about. I didn't want to do these things to simply appease my so-called guilty feelings, as was my usual routine.

Those so-called guilty feelings that had plagued me for years left in a brief moment of time. They just flew away into the graveyard of guilty feelings, never to be felt again. I mean it. This is not some kind of Evangelical Christian exaggeration, and let's be honest, sometimes Evangelical Christians have been known to exaggerate. Those feelings associated with guilt and condemnation have never returned to my life. I know where I stand with God. I know where I will spend eternity and with whom. I know I stand before the God of both the spiritual and material universe as a saved, innocent man. I am innocent of all charges rightly due me. My name has been transferred into what the book of Revelation calls the Lamb's Book of Life (Revelation 21:27) where, there is no sin or wrong-doing associated with my name.

One of the first things I did after that life-changing prayer was to go and buy myself a brand new very large print King James New Testament. I still have that Bible today. I will pass it onto my boys when I relocate to Heaven some day.

From that February, 1970, day onward, my passion in life has been to know what the Bible teaches, to understand the Biblical message, and to teach Biblical truth to others, but most of all, to allow the Biblical message to be implemented and realized in my life.

I am not saying I wasn't saved before that evening in February, 1970. I'm just saying that Jesus touched me in that short prayer that convinced me beyond any doubt that I was, in fact, forgiven of my sins and saved. Jesus removed the feelings associated with guilt that stifled my growth in the Lord, and, He can do the same for you. Feelings of guilt and condemnation work against the Holy Spirit's activity in one's life. They are not from God. Such feelings and emotions are purely humanistic and have no place in the life of the Christian. I was no longer inflicted with a life of condemnation.

Look at what the apostle Paul wrote just after he admitted that he still, even though he was saved, had to battle with his sinful nature. Romans 8:1 and 2 say this:

> "Therefore, there is now no condemnation for those who are in Christ Jesus, because through Christ Jesus the law of the Spirit who gives life has set you free from the law of sin and death."

If I was truly saved prior to that day in February, 1970, only Jesus knew. I certainly did not know for sure, and if I did not know for sure, then my so-called Christian life was next to meaningless. No wonder I was a lukewarm Christian.

6
The Holy Spirit

The following year, in 1971, I started hearing people talk about the Holy Spirit and speaking in tongues. All the things I was hearing were completely foreign to me, because, even though our church believed in the Holy Spirit's activity in the life of a Christian, our church did not believe in speaking in tongues in the sense in which I was hearing. Our church only believed that tongues were a valid gift of the Spirit today if the tongues were miraculously spoken on the mission field. In that sense of the word, the missionary would speak the gospel message in a language he did not know or learn. It would be a miracle language, the language of those the missionary was attempting to evangelize. They called that Acts 2 style tongues.

Our church believed that the original tongues that were spoken in Acts 2 actually preached the gospel to those who heard them. That is to say, the crowd of people from all parts of the known world, who heard the tongues, heard the gospel preached to them in their own language via the tongues. That was why they believed Acts 2 style tongues were a miracle language to be spoken, only on the mission field. Allow me to suggest that is a poor interpretation of Acts 2 style tongues.

The tongues that the one hundred and twenty newly-filled with the Holy Spirit people spoke in Acts 2 did not preach the gospel message to those who heard them. In fact, according to Acts 2:11, the tongues were a declaration "of the wonders of God." I do not believe "the wonders of God" was the gospel. If it was, then why did Peter have to repeat the gospel message in the very first Christian sermon ever preached, as seen in Acts 2? If the tongues were the proclamation of the gospel, Peter's preaching of the gospel would have been redundant.

The idea of tongues intrigued me immensely. People were telling me about this experience they called the "Baptism in the Holy Spirit." From what I had been told, this was something I, and others, felt I needed in my life, and so I set out on a journey to find this experience. Those promoting this experience called it "a second work of grace." The first work of grace was our salvation experience, being born again, or as I call it, "initial salvation."

The teaching concerning the Baptism of the Holy Spirit, for those who do not know, is what separates Pentecostal style Evangelical Christians from non-Pentecostal style Evangelical Christians. Don't you love all of these various Christian designations? Well, just for the record, I'm not a big fan of all of these designations.

During the March break from school in 1971, when I was in grade thirteen, I went on a trip to Lexington, Kentucky with three of my friends. Jim, Marlene, Dawne, and myself, visited a place called Christ Centre. It was located in a large, outdated, elementary school, in mid-town Lexington. The timing of this trip took place in the midst of what had been called the "Jesus People Movement," and those operating this ministry were definitely Jesus People. The building was not only an outreach centre for various ministries, but a commune in which some of the Jesus People could live.

Just in case you don't know, Jesus People, as they were called in the 1960's and 1970's, were newly saved young people, mostly from the drug infested hippie culture of the day.

It was in one of the classrooms of this restored school for Jesus, in a Tuesday evening gathering of believers, that I asked Jesus for this experience everyone was calling the "Baptism in the Spirit." Okay, not everyone was excited about this experience. A number of the adults in the church in which I was raised warned me against speaking in tongues and all of the damage it could do. For the life of me, I thought that if Jesus had some kind of a gift He wanted to give me, I would gladly, and thankfully, take it. I'd take anything He wanted to give me.

The meeting was like something that I had never seen or experienced. The room was packed with old and young men and women alike; from long haired young guys in torn jeans to bald headed senior men in suits. One over-weight man was actually sitting on the window sill because of lack of space for him to sit in the room. To see such a variety of people squeezed all together in the same room in the name of the Lord Jesus was amazing. I wasn't used to this. I was used to church life being segregated into babies, children, teenagers, college and career youths, newly married couples, middle-aged people, and seniors. Here we were, all of us, in the aforementioned room worshipping Jesus, without any prejudice or concern about someone looking different than us.

The worship was what impressed me most. At one point during the gathering some people began to quietly sing in tongues. The spiritual song grew in intensity and volume until it died down into a few minutes of quiet peacefulness. I had never heard that in my entire life. It left me with a great sense of God's peace. It was beautiful. It was soothing. It was simply worshipful. What I was seeing before my very eyes made me want this experience called the "Baptism in the Spirit" more than ever.

The meeting finally came to a conclusion. Those who wanted prayer were encouraged to stay behind, so I stayed behind to be prayed for. I was nervous. I admit that. Those preparing to pray for me attempted to calm my nerves by telling me that was natural. After explaining a few things to me, some brothers in the Lord laid their hands on me to receive this experience they called the "Baptism in the Holy Spirit."

I was anticipating an awesome experience with Jesus, but nothing happened. I repeat, absolutely nothing happened. I felt no empowerment. I felt no miraculous presence of the Holy Spirit. I just felt nothing, but a heavy dose of unexpected disappointment.

Someone told me that I needed to accept what I was asking Jesus for by faith. That meant I was to tell myself that I had received what I was asking for, even though I didn't appear to have received it. I've sense learned that receiving anything from Jesus doesn't require mind games like that. One either receives something from Jesus or one doesn't receive something from Jesus. I don't think it is all that complicated.

I went home from Kentucky disappointed, and discouraged because I did not receive what I really wanted. One of my friends, namely Robert, had gone to Elim Bible Institute and College, in Lima, New York, U.S.A. the same week I went to Kentucky. To my amazement and astonishment, he returned home praying in tongues. I could not believe that he had received what I wanted. Both of us knew nothing about these things prior to that March holiday, in 1971.

I asked Robert how someone like me could speak in tongues. In jesting, and he was jesting, he said that if I said the word "halleluiah" real fast ten times, my tongue would flip over and I would start speaking in tongues right away.

I didn't try Robert's, off-the-cuff in jest, suggestion. Neither did I try a couple other suggestions from other people.

One brother in the Lord told me to invent my own tongues. It could be any old homemade sound that I could come up with. If I would just step out in what they called faith, and speak my own invented tongues, then, Jesus would honour my effort of faith and give me the real thing. I didn't try that either. There is no hint in the Bible that we are to invent a gift of the Holy Spirit in our own human effort. Actually, if you read Galatians, chapter 3, you will see that the apostle Paul tells us not to live our faith by our own human effort. Tongues are a supernatural gift of the Spirit. Anything we do that attempts to twist the Holy Spirits arm in these matters hinders His purpose in our lives. Galatians 3:3 says this:

> "Are you so foolish? After beginning by means of the Spirit, are you now trying to finish by means of the flesh?"

I was not so foolish, as Paul intimated about his Galatian readers.

Then there was the time at a Pentecostal church altar where myself and someone else were seeking the Baptism in the Spirit, accompanied by speaking in tongues. The pastor told the person kneeling beside me to copy, or repeat, his tongues. Now that is utterly ridiculous. There was no way I would copy someone's so-called valid tongues and attempt to claim they came from the Holy Spirit. Lots of crazy things take place in the Christian world sometimes. I refused to participate in that crazy scheme.

A couple weeks after my visit to Kentucky, while in a small prayer meeting, one funny little word escaped from my lips while I was praying. "This must be a word in tongues," or so I thought. I certainly did not invent this word. I was really happy. Finally, I had received tongues, even if it was just one word.

A month past and discouragement set in once again. How could one unfamiliar word be a valid supernatural gift of the Holy Spirit? It must have been some kind of psychosomatic thing. Despite my questioning and discouragement, every time I was in a prayer meeting, I would pray this one funny little word, until one day, it happened again. Another word slipped off my tongue. Once again I was happy, at least for a week or so, but as usual, discouragement returned to burden my non-tongues-speaking soul. Over and over I asked myself how two unfamiliar words could be valid Biblical tongues. Maybe I just wanted it so bad that my mind was playing games with me. Still, I would pray these two words when in prayer meetings, until, in yet another meeting, it happened again. A third word came spewing from my mouth. "I now had three whole words in tongues," or so I hoped.

In the summer of 1971, I only had those three words of what I sometimes thought was tongues. I almost gave up on tongues for good during July and August of that year. I would let the Pentecostals pray in tongues all their little hearts desired. I, on the other hand, would stick to my native language of English. I had no real problem praying in English.

It was September, 1971, in my bedroom. I was all alone with my guitar in hand. While singing worship songs to the Lord it finally happened, and it happened for real. After deciding to sing those three so-called words of tongues to Jesus, all of a sudden there was a massive explosion of tongues as I sang in the powerful presence of the Lord. It was like a flood, a flood of a language I had never known. Those three words morphed into sentences and paragraphs. On and on it went. For at least forty five minutes or more I prayed and sang in tongues in the presence of Jesus, my Saviour and Lord. Was this the real thing? There is no doubt in my mind that it was, definitely, the real thing. There have been very few, if any, days since then that I have not prayed in tongues.

7
Redefining My Experience

As Christians, we should constantly be learning from the Word of God, the Bible. This means that at certain times in our maturity as a Christian we must relearn what we have thought to be Biblical truth but wasn't. We might well have to re-adjust our unbiblical thinking, which would result in redefining what we have experienced to match what the Bible teaches. I did just that concerning the Baptism in the Holy Spirit.

Don't misunderstand what I have just said. I did not say you have to throw out and reject the validity of your personal experience. I'm just saying that you may have to re-interpret it in light of what the Bible says.

Why did nothing seemingly happen to me in Kentucky when those people prayed for me? Should I have accepted what I asked Jesus for by faith, as they told me? Should I have tried to trick my mind into believing I spoke in tongues when in fact I had not? One of my friends told me years ago that he called such thinking "mental gymnastics." I'm not into being a mental gymnast.

Back in 1972 I did try what is often called Hyper Faith for a while, although those who embrace Hyper Faith teaching would tell me that you can't just try it for a year. Hyper Faith is both believing and acting that you have received from God what you have asked God for, even though the outward appearance suggests that you have not received what you have asked for. Anyway, I bought myself a very small print New Testament by faith. I mean it had print so small that most people could not read it, even if they used their glasses to read. I just knew that this step of faith would prompt Jesus to heal my eyes.

I looked at that Bible every day for months on end. I strained my eyes in an attempt to read the Word of the Lord, but day after day, I could not read that very fine, small, print. I still have that Bible today and I still can't see well enough to read it. I would dare say that you could probably not read it as well. I've learned that Jesus is my Lord, not my servant. He does not bow His knee to my every wish, request, or expectation. I bow my knee to His will, His wishes, and His expectations. He is Lord, not me.

The reason why nothing happened to me in that Tuesday evening meeting in Kentucky is this. Those praying for me believed I needed to receive the Holy Spirit into my life. The way in which this could happen would be if I received what they called the Baptism in the Spirit. To them, this experience is what is called a second work of grace. That is to say, it is secondary to being saved, or, being born again, however you want to say it. Their thinking, that inspired their prayer, was the problem.

What I have since come to understand is that the Baptism in the Spirit is the same thing as receiving the Holy Spirit when one first gets saved, or as my dad used to call it, being born again of the Spirit of God. This experience called the Baptism in the Spirit is not a second work of grace, as Pentecostals believe it to be. It is actually one's salvation experience. So, when those people prayed for me to receive the Baptism in the Spirit, meaning I would receive the Holy Spirit subsequent to my initial salvation; that could not have happened. I had already received what they called the Baptism in the Spirit when I received the Holy Spirit in my life when I first got saved. I had already received what I was asking for, because, the Baptism in the Holy

Spirit is the reception of the Spirit into one's life at one's initial salvation.

If all of this sounds way to confusing for you, and for many it does sound confusing, you can read my book entitled "Pentecost Revisited." There you will read what I understand to be the Biblical truth on this matter.

If you want to pigeonhole me into a doctrinal box, which I don't really think is all that important; I am Pentecostal by experience but certainly not by doctrine. If you, like me, are truly a born of the Spirit believer, accept me as one as well. We can differ on many issues, but the basic truths of the gospel should be understood by all of us alike. Far too often Christians separate over that which I call secondary Biblical issues. That should never be the case.

One thing that I did not have prior to September, 1971, was the gift of tongues. That gift I received over a period of a few months in 1971, culminating in the experience in my bedroom that I mentioned above. That glorious occasion was not the Baptism in the Spirit as many would call it. It was a special experience I had with the Lord Jesus in which He gave me one of His spiritual gifts. Since then I have had many experiences like that with Jesus. I do not call them Baptisms in the Spirit number two, number three, number four, number five, and so on. I call them times in which God has poured His Spirit out on me in a fresh way. These are what I call Acts 4 experiences. I call these special powerful encounters with the Holy Spirit Acts 4 experiences because the same people who received the Spirit of God by means of being baptized or immersed in Him in Acts 2 were re-immersed, or baptized, in God's Spirit again in Acts 4.

8
Spiritually Schizophrenic

It was in 1973, when Jerry B. Walker, a well known preacher with a healing ministry came to Toronto, Ontario. I, and my friend Gerry, drove to Toronto to attend one of his healing meetings. At the end of his sermon he invited those of us who desired healing to come forward for prayer. I walked to the front of the sanctuary and stood with others in what is traditionally called a healing line. I had stood in many, and I mean many, of these lines before while being raised in the church. My dad made sure of that I had ample opportunities to have my legally blind eyes healed.

On two previous occasions I attended Katherine Coolman's healing meetings in Pittsburgh, Pennsylvania. She was a real famous lady with a healing ministry in the 1960's and 1970's. Although many claimed to be healed in her meetings, on both occasions I return home, unhealed.

Anyway, back to Gerry B. Walker's healing line. When it came time for him to pray for me, he didn't even pray. He said nothing. He just placed one of his hands over my eyes and laughed. That's it. He laughed and went onto the next person in line. What was that all about? I interpreted his laughter as a laugh of victory, even though there was no hint of a victorious outcome to his non-prayer.

The next year Walker came to our home town and once again, I stood in his healing line. There was no laughter this time. He did actually pray for me when he approached me in the line, but, his prayer was not one of those seemingly, heavy-duty, Holy Spirit inspired, prayers. He just prayed; "Lord, help my buddy," and then moved on to the next poor soul who needed divine healing. That left me scratching my head in wonder. What did that apparently unspiritual prayer mean? "Lord, help my buddy." Was that the best he can do for me?

There is one thing I know about Gerry B. Walker and his healing line I stood in while in Toronto. When he approached me, there was absolutely nothing about me that would have told him that I had an eyesight problem. I did not tell him anything about me. I said nothing. Anyone who simply looks at me cannot tell that I am legally blind. How, then, could he have known I could not see well, as he placed one of his hands over my eyes and then laughed? I concluded it was the Lord Jesus who had clued him in on my eyesight issue, but, why he laughed is anyone's guess. Maybe he saw me in the next life with perfect vision. That would produce a victorious laugh. Or, maybe he saw me effectively serving Jesus, even with my disability. That would be worth a laugh of victory too.

I say all of the above to say this. When it comes to the healing of my eyes, I have learned to relax and just trust Jesus, no matter the outcome. I am not bugging Him on a daily basis for my healing, as some do. I am not claiming or demanding my healing from Him, as others do. I am not acting, in faith, as if I am already healed when in fact I am not healed, as some suggest. If Jesus heals my eyes, I would be more than happy and grateful, and, I would certainly know that I am healed. There would be no question about that. If He chooses not to heal me, which is His prerogative, you won't see me getting bent out of shape over my non-healing.

I have had countless people try to heal my eyes through various ways and means over the decades. People have prophesied all sorts of things about my healing, all of these prophecies being different in their content. People have tried to cast demons out of me. I've been in healing lines and deliverance-from-demon lines. I, and others, have prayed and fasted for my healing. I have claimed from the Lord, along with others, my healing. Whatever kind of healing formula one can come up with, and there is no Biblical formula for healing, it's been tried on me.

If I have believed all of prophecies spoken over me about my healing, and, if I had embraced all that people have told me that I should do to get healed, I would indeed be spiritually schizophrenic. That I choose not to be.

There is one thing that many people over the years have consistently told me, and that is this. "You may be legally blind, but, you certainly are not spiritually blind." If that is a prophetic word, I will choose to accept that one.

9
The Jesus People Movement

In 1971, I, and three of my Christian friends moved into a farm house just outside of Trenton, Ontario, Canada. Trenton is about twelve miles west of Belleville, the city wherein I live today, in 2019. We had met up with the group called the Children of God, who unknowing to us at first, was a pretty bad cult. One thing we soon discovered about this group that validated the designation of cult was that their attractive young girls would prostitute themselves in the hope of winning as many sexually active young guys to the Lord as could be possible. I'm sure you would agree with me, that is no way to win men for Jesus.

Some of my friends left their family and friends to join the Children of God, or the COG, as we called them. My friends and I were actually the group that invited this cult, and that by mistake, into the province of Ontario. Two very close friends of mine joined the Children of God and then left after two months because the cult's leaders wanted to ship my friends newly born baby to Texas to be raised while her parents dedicated their lives to preaching Jesus on the streets. Some of my other friends stayed in the group for years, even decades. It was all about satanic mind control, all in the name of Jesus.

It was in the midst of all this turmoil over the Children of God, and the turmoil included a fist-fight on the front steps of a Pentecostal church building, that my friends and I decided to live together in what was commonly called a Christian Commune back in those years. This was the beginning of the Jesus People Movement, a valid revival of God, in our region of Ontario, Canada.

We experienced many exciting times in the first half of the 1970's. There are far too many things to recall in this format. We preached Jesus on the streets, which included being punched and pushed around by drunks. We preached Jesus in bars, schools, a college, parks, and churches. We preached anywhere and everywhere we could find to preach. Every conceivable place to proclaim the gospel of Jesus was fair game for us.

One day we gathered a crowd of kids in a locker area at a local high school and started preaching. The crowd of kids grew to the extent that it caused much commotion and congestion. The principle of the school told us to stop preaching. One of my friends told the principle that he, or no one else, had the authority to prevent us from preaching the gospel in the name of the Lord Jesus Christ. Taken aback, the principle replied by telling us that we didn't have to stop preaching. He just preferred we preach in a more conducive and less congested format, so, he permitted us to preach in a designated room after school was over. We could preach until our hearts were content. He announced our meeting on the school's public address system. The classroom was jammed-packed, full of students and teachers alike. It was standing room only. We could never do anything like that these days. Christianity and the public school system just do not mix any more.

We had a couple of coffee house ministries in the early 1970's. On one occasion someone came in from off the street. He was drunk. He punched me, causing me to fly over a table and onto the floor. While attempting to get back onto my feet, he kicked me in the head, and back onto the floor I flew. It was like an old-time, cowboy style, bar-room brawl, except I never got to throw a punch.

We had a Jesus People News Paper along with our own tracts that we would hand out to young people wherever we would find them. The Jesus Paper was called "Into Jesus." Young people back then were "into" all sorts of things. They were into drinking, into drugs, and of course, into free sex, but not us. We were "into Jesus."

Once we had a chance to speak about Jesus to a college class. The teacher was Jewish. She seriously questioned our faith in Jesus, who we called, "her Messiah." She obviously differed with us on that point. We gave the class, including the teacher, opportunity to give their lives to Jesus. As far as I know, that Jewish lady teacher did not become a believer. She was, however, killed in a car accident the following week.

We led a rock band to Jesus who was booked to play in a local bar for a month or so. We would sit in and listen to their music, and once their set was over, we would go upstairs, pray, read the Bible, and share a bottle of wine with the members of the group.

On one occasion my friend Jim and I were called into the local government customs and immigration office for questioning. We had seen police cars slowly drive by our farm house a few times every day. We found out that the police and the local government immigration officer thought we were a part of the Children of God cult, who they believed, were in Canada illegally. After we were interrogated for an hour or so, the officer was convinced we were not covert members of the Children of God. As I got up from my chair and headed out the door, I handed the immigration officer a Jesus tract and told him that Jesus could save Him. I did have a good measure of boldness back then, or, should I call it a naive lack of wisdom.

On another occasion I and another brother in the Lord got to share our testimonies in a world religions class in one of our high schools in town. I believe we were filled with the Spirit as we shared our stories. One student, thinking I was high on drugs, asked me what I was high on. I told him that I was high on the Holy Spirit. I guess you could say that was an accurate portrayal but I wouldn't use that terminology today.

As I have said, there are far too many events to relate to you from what I call "my Jesus People days." They were one of the most exciting times of my life. We learned a lot back then. We learned how to share Jesus, what Christian community means, and along the way, the foundations of our faith were greatly strengthened.

Me, in my Jesus People days.

10
Demons

In and around 1972, one of my friends read this little, red-covered, book entitled "Out In The Name Of Jesus." I can no longer remember who wrote it, but it has probably been long since out of print, and for that, I am quite glad. Some of us adopted its teaching concerning how to successfully cast demons out of people. Back in those days, what was called the "Deliverance Movement" was taking off all over the place in the Charismatic Movement. So my friends and I followed the trend. I choose the word "trend" with considerable thought. Some Evangelical Christians have the tendency to follow the latest trend. They jump on the next bandwagon passing through their town. They follow the newest Christian fad, and, there are such things as Christian fads. So here we were, believing what this little red book told us about demons. We, thus, saw demons in all sorts of places where they most likely were not.

My friend got it all started when he was walking his girlfriend home from school one day. While cutting through a secluded field, he attempted to cast a demon out of her. She freaked out, as we would say back then. He attributed her reaction to her being under the influence, if not possessed, by a demon. The casting out of demons became high on our list of Christian activities.

We would often spend eight or more exhausting and mind-boggling hours after a Sunday morning meeting attempting to cast demons out of people. It got quite tiring at times, as you might imagine. Well, maybe you can't imagine it, if you have not been so occupied with demons as we were.

On one occasion we supposedly threw out one hundred and eighteen demons out of one girl. The last evil spirit to leave was a lying spirit, or so he said. The little red book taught that we must ask for the name of the demon before we could cast him out, and that we did. This demon told us that he was a lying spirit. I questioned him by asking if he was in fact a lying spirit. How could we know if he was telling us the truth, if he was a lying spirit? Things got very strange at times.

For the record, we did list all of the names of these demons. Did we really cast one hundred and eighteen demons out of this girl? Well, that is questionable. Did we cast any demon out of her? Well, that might be debatable as well. There is one thing I know. At one point during the whole process, it took one of us holding her head down, one holding one arm down, one holding her other arm down, and me, sitting on her ankles, just to keep her from going crazy and running from our presence. Who knows where she would have ended up. She literally had the strength to lift her legs with me on her ankles, and then, throw me onto the floor. You try doing that some day. It's a difficult, if not impossible thing to do. The next day I had an arm-wrestle with her, and it took no effort on my part to win the arm-wrestling contest. How she got so strong during our time of casting demons out of her is a wonder. There was something going on there.

On one occasion I was sick with the flu. A couple of friends took me down to a quiet spot by the river to cast a demon of flu out of me. I went home sick as ever. Apparently, I did not have a demon of flu, or else my friends did not have the ability to cast the demon of flu out of me. Is there really a demon of flu? Is the flu demonic or a simple illness? You can answer that question for yourself.

I will not labour you with the time we chased a girl through a couple of streets and tackled her to the ground in the middle of a baseball game. I won't tell you how she was about to stab us with a butcher knife. All that I will tell you is that the little, red-covered, book, was somewhat unbiblical in its approach to demons.

The Bible does speak of demons, and how they can influence people, but to do all that we did, is beyond the boundary of Scripture, or so I believe. We did learn some lessons from our over-emphasis. One lesson I believe we learned was that a born-again-of-the-Spirit Christian cannot be possessed by a demon.

Don't get me wrong. Our over-emphasis in this matter does not mean that I no longer believe in the existence of demons, because I do believe in their reality. That being said, not all that is called demonic by some is demonic. I know that for sure. Our human, sinful, nature, has caused many problems in our lives. We don't have to blame Satan for all of our problems. We must blame ourselves for many of life's difficulties. James 1:14 tells us that we don't need the devil's help in causing us to give into sin's temptation. James said this:

"... but each person is tempted when they are dragged away by their own evil desire and enticed."

Let's put the blame where it really lies, and that is with us. We can't blame the devil or demons for every negative thing that transpires in our lives.

11
Elim Bible Institute And College

In June, 1975, my friend Glenn and mentor in the Lord, suggested that I attend Elim Bible Institute and College in Lima, New York, U.S.A.. I told him that if I were to attend Elim, I would like to do it when my friend Robert was attending, so I would at least know one person at an unfamiliar college. He had one year left in his three year program when Glenn spoke this suggestion to me. Although I had never been at Elim, Glenn knew the President of the school, David Edwards, quite well.

At the time I was working in a dirty, smelly, old factory called Stewart Warner, here in Belleville, Ontario. I could not get Glenn's suggestion out of my mind for three entire days as I worked away on my buffing machine. As a result, I decided to enrol at Elim, located just south of Rochester, New York.

It was a last minute decision and lots had to be accomplished in time for me to attend classes at the end of August, and that included the all-important student visa so I could enter and live in the United States. I was not sure that all that needed to be done could be done on time, but if Jesus wanted me at Elim, He could certainly pull that off, and He did. It was a miracle. I'm sure you know, that government, and especially the American government, does not move very fast.

I spent two good years at Elim. I learned many things there that I most likely could not have learned elsewhere. My Elim days have had a lasting and profound effect on my life. My appreciation for the Word of God grew with a better understanding of how to study the Bible.

While at Elim I learned that there are many other very good Christians that may not think exactly like I think, or, even as you think. That has made me more tolerant of other Christians. We must never disagree on the basic issues of Scripture, and that would include the message of salvation and who Jesus is, but, when it comes to what I call secondary Biblical issues, we should know why we believe in them and we should not separate from others who may think differently.

It is a sad fact of history, but Christians have divided over these secondary issues far too often over the centuries. It has damaged our effectiveness as the church that has been called to represent Jesus to our culture in a unified representation. Jesus prayed that we would all be one, just as He and His Father are one (John 17:11). We have sure messed up that prayer.

The message we read in Romans 14 and 1 Corinthians 14 is about diversity within unity. We are all distinct individuals with our personal, God-given, calling in life, but, we are to live out our diversity in one unified format. That is church. You might want to read those chapters over for yourself.

I also met my first wife at Elim. Cathy was the reason why I never returned to finish the third and final year of the pastoral theology and ministry course I was enrolled in. Instead of receiving a diploma for Christian ministry, I obtained a certificate for the ministry of marriage.

Cathy and I were married on June 25, 1977, and had two wonderful sons. They are; Jeremy Lee (born June, 20, in 1983, in Richmond, Virginia) and, Jonathan Robert (born February 7, 1988, in Belleville, Ontario, Canada).

In short, the most beneficial things I received from my Bible college days were: the introduction to the various tools to study the Bible, and, the people I met, which included Cathy, my first wife. Obviously, without Cathy in my life, I would not be the father of my two sons.

You may notice that I call Cathy my first wife. I'm not a polygamous, so don't worry about that. I've only had one wife at a time. If you keep reading, you will learn about my second, and final, wife.

You can learn about Elim Bible Institute and College by visiting their web site at https://www.elim.edu/ .

12
The Shepherding Movement

While I was away at Elim Bible Institute and College, our small church fellowship got connected with Bob Mumford, Charles Simpson, Don Basham, Derek Prince, and Ern Baxter. These men were leaders of what was then called the "Shepherding Movement," which was a sub-movement within the Charismatic Movement of the 1960's and 1970's. I've commented on the Shepherding Movement a few times on my web site (www.stevesweetman.com). You can search for some articles on this movement there and learn more about my thoughts on the movement.

If you are not familiar with what I have called the Charismatic Movement, it was a revival movement where the Holy Spirit came into the lives of many people in various church denominations, especially in mainline, or, older denominational churches, during the 1960's and 1970's.

I settled back into Belleville after two years at Elim Bible Institute and College in the spring of 1977 as a new husband and into a restructured church family. We had asked a pastor, or shepherd, as we called him back then, to come and lead us here in Belleville. Jim, and his wife and four children, moved from Vienna, Virginia to Belleville in 1977. The Shepherding Movement was born in Eastern, Canada. Once again we were the instigators of something new coming to our region of Canada concerning church.

Those days were good days. We had many exciting times. Although there were some abuses concerning overly-authoritative shepherds in the Shepherding Movement in the United States, we never really experienced any abuses here in Belleville. We promoted having personal, supportive, relationships in the Body of Christ. The church is not a building. It is not simply an organizational structure. It is a group of born-again-of-the-Spirit believers who have been called alongside others in the Body of Christ. The church is Christians relating to one another in Christian community, as each member seeks to serve Jesus, both individually and collectively with those Jesus has place them alongside.

I never fully embraced all aspects of the shepherding teaching, but I did embrace those to whom Jesus had placed me alongside in the Body of Christ. They were, and still are, a major blessing in my life.

My passport photo in 1980

13
Moving To Virginia

Our pastor Jim, or shepherd, as he was called back then, who had moved from Virginia with his family to care for us, decided to return to Virginia in 1980 after experiencing a major heart attack. As was often the case in the Shepherding Movement, sheep, meaning, those under the care of a shepherd, would follow their shepherd when he relocated, and that we did. I and my wife moved to Vienna, Virginia, with Jim and his wife and family. We packed all that we had into a U-Hall trailer and off we went to America in August, 1980.

The day we drove down highway 401 here in Ontario, with all of our possessions packed into a U-Haul trailer, felt extraordinarily weird. I was leaving Belleville, the city in which I was born and raised. I was leaving Canada to live in a foreign country. Okay, it's not as foreign as other countries around the world that one might experience. Canada and America are more alike than different. That being said, it still felt strange.

What I was beginning to miss most as we drove down the highway, and, what I did miss most after settling into Virginia, was my friends, my city, and, listening to Montreal Expos baseball games on the radio. I had become a huge baseball fan and the Expos were my team of choice. I had to reluctantly listen to Baltimore Orioles baseball on the radio while living in Northern Virginia.

Vienna, where we relocated our lives, is a suburb of Washington D C. It was quite an exhilarating place to live, at least for me, a small city boy. The phrase "a fast pace of living" is an understatement when it comes to living in a Washington D C suburb.

While living in Vienna, I learned, or should I say, had no other choice but to learn, to like American style politics and the Washington Redskins football team. When it came to the Washington Redskins, you were a big fan, and if you weren't, well, you had a limited number of friends. Redskin fans are obsessively dedicated to their team.

We lived in Vienna for about eight months and then decided to move south to Richmond, Virginia. There we would become part of another related church family within the Shepherding Movement.

We spent more than three years in Richmond, being very involved in church activities, and in the lives to whom Jesus had placed us alongside in the Body of Christ. As I have said, in those days, we were all encouraged to come under the care of a shepherd. We were also encouraged to shepherd, or care for, others as well. I had four families that I was responsible to care for. We believed that most of the work of the Lord was done outside of the confines of church meetings, a concept that is sometimes lost in our western-world church in our generation. I still believe that the most effective work of the Lord is accomplished outside of church meetings and church buildings.

In 1978 I spoke a Sunday message to a local church congregation. I asked this question. "If you did not have this building you gather in, and, if you had no regular scheduled meetings, would you still have a church?" It was a question that few, if any, had ever asked or thought about. I dare say that in most cases, a group of people who consider themselves a church would not exist if they did not have a building to meet in and regularly scheduled meetings to attend. This would be the case because their church activities are centered around their building and their meetings and not personal relationships. Personal relationships are fundamental to all that church is.

I believe that the Biblical teaching concerning church has been lost in much of our western-world, Evangelical Church these days. By building relationships with those to whom Jesus has placed us within church, we could properly care for those in our charge and that is what we attempted to do in the Shepherding Movement. That is what I did while living in Richmond, Virginia.

The biggest event that took place while living in Richmond came in June, 1983. It was then, my first son, Jeremy Lee, was born into our family. That day still ranks as one of the most memorable days of my entire life. I had talked to Jeremy for months while he resided within his mother prior to his birth. Within minutes of arriving into the daylight of the hospital room, I was holding him in my arms. He looked up at me, and as if to ask, "So you're the guy who has been talking to me all of these months?"

Within a year, for various reasons, we decided to return to Canada. That was June, 1984. We lived in Virginia for four years. Those were good years. I met people, visited places, and did many things while living there that I would not have otherwise met, visited, or have gotten to do. It was definitely a growing and learning experience for me. I have no regrets experiencing the American south.

Do I believe it was God's will for us to have moved to the United States in 1980? To be perfectly honest, I really don't know the answer to that question for sure. Much good did come from that move, and some not so good, but, all in all, I learned a lot. I am just not one hundred percent sure it was God's will. If it wasn't, He sure made the best of a mistake, which in the reality of things, is probably often the case with us all. As Christians, we don't always get things right, but the Lord still is with us, and He works with us for His good, despite our mistakes. I am sure of that.

14
Politics

As mentioned above, in 1980, my wife and I moved to Vienna, Virginia, a Washington D C suburb. One cannot live in or around Washington D C without encountering the rough and tumble world of American style politics. It is simply unavoidable. After my friend took me on a tour through Washington, which included, the Capitol Building, the White House, and the various museums, the political bug, or maybe I should call it a virus, infected me.

One day my friend and I sat in the United States senate chamber. We listened intently to Democratic Senator Edward Kennedy expound on what was then called the "Peace Movement." There was a movement among many Americans back then to end the Cold War with the Soviet Union, and that was what Senator Kennedy was expounding upon with great conviction.

Ironically, it was not a Democrat that helped bring the Cold War to an end. If you are of my age, you will remember these memorable words spoken by then Republican President, Ronald Reagan. These words have defined his presidency. While in West Berlin, on June 12, 1987, President Reagan stood beside the Berlin Wall and shouted out these memorable words. "Gorbachev, tare down this wall." It wasn't too long after the utterance of these words that the great dividing wall fell in a heap of rubble. People were literally picking of its pieces for a souvenir. The fall of this great wall precipitated the fall of the Soviet Union. Will the Soviet Union ever rise from its heap of ashes? It might be in that process right now, as many believe Ezekiel, chapters 38 and 39 allude to. I won't get involved in the end-time debate over those chapters. I've done that in my commentary on the book of Ezekiel that you can find on my web site.

As far as presidents go, Ronald Reagan was my favourite. I lived within a few miles of the U.S. Capitol Building where he was inaugurated as the 40th President of the United States in January, 1981. I vividly recall that day as I watched the proceedings on television.

After moving to Richmond, Virginia, I was, you might say, caught up in what was called "the Conservative Christian Right." This was a Christian political movement, led by such men as Pat Robertson (founder of the Christian Broadcasting Network) and Jerry Falwell (president of Liberty University). Robertson lived in Virginia Beach, Virginia. Falwell lived in Lynchburg, Virginia. I lived in Richmond, right in between Virginia Beach and Lynchburg. How could I have not gotten caught up in the Conservative Christian Right, that was out to bring America back to its so-called Christian roots? My participation just seemed the religiously correct thing to do at the time.

During the 1982 U.S. mid-term election I was the canvassing co-ordinator for the Republican Party in our area of Richmond. That meant I organized people to go door to door and pass out pamphlets promoting people to vote for the local Republican candidate for congress. That I did, even though I, myself, could not vote in the election because I was not an American citizen. That is how involved I became in the political process.

When my wife, my son, and I, returned to Canada in 1984 I joined the newly founded Christian Heritage Party. Like the Conservative Christian Right in America, those in the Christian Heritage Party wanted to return Canada to its, also so-called, Christian roots.

I know longer believe that either Canada or the United States could be considered Christian when they were founded. Both countries had severe national sins, that in my opinion, disqualified them as being Christian nations. Besides that, a close study of the history of nations in the Bible tells me that no nation has ever been, or ever will be, Christian. All nations are anti-God to one degree or another. All nations will fall to God's judgment as seen in Revelation, chapters 18 and 19.

Were Canada and the United States influenced by Biblical thought? They were influenced by some religious thought that was not necessarily Biblical. They were also influenced by some valid Biblical thought as well, but, simply being influenced by religious or Biblical thinking makes no one, or no nation, Christian.

I had the privilege of asking Ern Baxter, a prominent Bible teacher in the 1970's and 1980's about Pat Roberson's attempt to win the presidency of the United States in 1988.

His answer was impactful. It began to change my thinking concerning Christians and politics. He said that if Pat Robertson becomes president of the United States, he must acknowledge that he has demoted himself from being a preacher of the gospel of the Lord Jesus Christ to being president of the most powerful nation on earth. Now that is a major demotion. Baxter's response to my question is well worth thinking over, and that I did. I now believe that my first allegiance is to the Kingdom of God, not the kingdoms of men, and that includes Canada, the nation in which I live.

If you would like to read more of my thoughts on this issue, you can read them in my book entitled, "The Politics Of God And The Bible."

15
A New Home

In June, 1984, my wife, our one year old son, and I, returned to Belleville, Ontario, ready to start life all over again. With no place to live we stored all of our possessions in my father's garage. He had to park his Cadillac, which he always (emphasis on the word "always") kept perfectly clean, in his driveway. Although he never said anything about that, I am pretty sure he was not real happy about his car losing its home for a couple of months

My wife, my son, and I, all slept on the floor in my mom and dad's basement. The first night back seemed very strange for me. While attempting to fall asleep, and I do mean attempting, my heart sank to my stomach, which began to twist and twirl around in knots. "What have we done?" I asked myself. "We're starting all over again with no jobs, no income, and no place to live. Was this God's will? Are we crazy? Have we made a mistake? What's going to happen to us now?" All of these questions and more, were nervously swirling around in my head.

If you are honest, as I am, I doubt that everything you have done in your life as a Christian and every choice you have made as a believer, was based on God's intended will for you. Sometimes we just have to admit that we get things wrong. Going to Virginia in the first place was questionable, as I have said. Were we following our shepherd or were we following Jesus. You might ask yourself whether you always follow Jesus or simply your own desired path. Whatever the case, I have no real regrets about moving to the United States, and, I absolutely have no regrets moving back to Canada. That, I believe was God's will.

Within a few days after returning to Belleville my friend Glenn suggested that we think about buying a house. "How could we buy a house?" I asked both Glenn and myself. We had no jobs, no income, and not enough money for a down-payment on a house. We would find it difficult to rent an apartment let alone buying a house. Even though it made no sense I did entertain Glenn's suggestion.

I set up an appointment to talk with a mortgage manager at a local bank. I asked her if she and the bank believed in creative financing, a term I had recently learned from a "get-rich-quick-through-real-estate" conference I had attended in Virginia. After hearing my story the lady mortgage manager calmly, but bluntly, answered. "Well Steve, I'm sorry to tell you, we are not that creative." I admit, that sounds a bit humorous. This simply meant that we needed a miracle, and not a mortgage. If we were to buy a house, Jesus would have to make it happen without the assistance of a bank, and that He did. I guess one doesn't always need a bank when he has Jesus. That certainly was the case in our situation.

To make a long miracle story short, we discovered that even though the bank was not creative, God still was, and always will be, creative. The Bible makes it clear that God, by His very nature, is creative. He did not stop creating at the end of what we call "the sixth day of Genesis 1." He did not put his feet up, so to speak, and sit back and relax. The last few chapters of the book of Revelation prove that God is always creative. There will come a time when God will undertake a massive, universal, creation scheme.

We purchased ourselves a townhouse. We needed about $8,500.00 to put down on the townhouse and pay the lawyer fees. We had $2,000.00 of our own money and the rest was given to us by family and our brothers and sisters in Christ. We bought a townhouse for $29,500.00. We assumed a $22,000.00 mortgage that we did not have to qualify for. I repeat, we did not have to qualify for that mortgage. We simply assumed the existing mortgage. If you can find that kind of mortgage today, you have found a miracle mortgage. No one knew that we had no jobs and no income. Can you believe that? We just signed a contract saying that we would continue to pay the monthly mortgage fees that the lady who we bought the house from had been paying.

We were buying that townhouse, paying less every month for the mortgage, taxes, and common costs, than our neighbours were paying to rent their townhouse. The combination of mortgage, taxes, and common costs for us totalled $315.00 a month. Our next-door, neighbours, were paying $550.00 a month to rent their townhouse, and that did not include utilities. I think we had quite a good deal, don't you think?

To make another long miracle story short, in the fall of 1986 we sold that townhouse for

$55,000.00, and we did so quickly in order to purchase the house we wanted; the house I now live in. If we would have been willing to wait it out, we could have easily gotten more money for our townhouse, but we did not want to wait. We wanted the house we were interested in.

During the two years we lived in that townhouse the prices of properties escalated to new heights, and they did so, very rapidly. The result was that we made about $31,000.00 on the sale of our townhouse. Through a couple of miracles we purchase the house that I live in today. We put $25,000.00 down on the house, paid the realtor and the lawyer and had $2,000.00 left over. That $2,000.00 was our initial $2,000.00 investment of our own money that we put towards the price of the townhouse. We got our initial investment back. How amazing that was. We were now in a house and still paying less every month than our old, next-door, neighbours were paying to rent their townhouse. Both our townhouse and the house that I am in today, are blessings, and really, miracles from God.

Within six years I would need another miracle to keep my house because of divorce, and that I received through a personal check for

$33,000.00. A number of years later, another miracle was needed to replace the shingles on our house, and that too, I received. This time I received a personal check for $7,100.00 from a different source. I certainly believe in miracles. Hopefully you do too.

16
Another Son

On February 7, 1988, in Belleville General Hospital, my second son, Jonathan Robert, came into this world. It was the very same hospital where I had been born, some thirty seven years earlier. Jonathan completed our small family. Two children in these times seem to be a reasonable number of children to raise into adulthood. Jonathan, like his brother Jeremy, was an easy child to raise. They have turned into two fine adult men. As I write these words in 2019, both of my sons work in successful careers in the field of computer and internet software development and design.

I can say from experience that the love of a father for his sons never fades. Despite the miles apart, sons are always their father's sons. My prayer is, and always will be, that I will see my Jeremy and Jonathan in the next life with Jesus.

In one real sense of the word, Jonathan was a miracle baby. In the summer of 1987 we could have easily lost him during my wife's pregnancy. After a day of major bleeding in July, 1987, the doctor told us that my wife most likely lost Jonathan's twin. Jonathan having a twin? That makes me curious. What would he or she have been like? I am sure two Jonathans would have been just as much of a joy to have as one Jonathan has been. Jonathan was, and still is, a blessing from God.

17
Our Church Closes

By 1987 our church here in Belleville had dwindled down to about five couples. We seemed to have stagnated, and what most would not do, we did. We jointly decided to close things down after seventeen plus years in existence. It was a sad day but there seemed to be no other choice to make.

Over those seventeen years I recall meeting in at least eighteen different locations, and that just for Sunday meetings. I'm not including mid-week meetings where we met in homes. That might well have been one of our problems concerning growth. Christians in North America are used to having their own building to meet in, but that was not our emphasis. Our emphasis was on relationships, not buildings.

Although we do not meet together any more on a consistent, organized, basis, we still remain good friends and brothers in Christ to this very day. The reason for our lasting friendship and brotherhood in Christ is because we were joined relationally, not organizationally, in the Body of Christ.

Just because a group of Christians disband organizationally, does not mean they should disband relationally. We knew better than that. Personal relationships are what church is all about. Organizational structures come and go, but the family of God endures forever. Organizations are merely a tool in the hands of the Lord. Sometimes organizations need to shut down. They have had their effective days and keeping them alive, even though they are really dead, is a waste of time, finances, and effort. Maintaining a dead church group is futile, and really, is unbiblical. This is part of the problem with many denominations that are now outdated. They have lost their present-day effectiveness. It's only pride or an unwillingness to change that keeps these dead organizations going.

If you read what Jesus said to the church at Ephesus, in Revelation, chapter 2, you will see that a church without the inspiring light of the Spirit of God is just a shell of a church, and, a shell of a church is not a New Testament church. So, we shut what was once called Koinonia Fellowship, and then, Quinte

Fellowship, down. We moved on with our lives.

18
Divorce

In and around 1988 and 1989, within a couple months of each other, both my best friend and my brother went through devastating marriage breakups. In both cases their wives had left them for no Biblical reason. Those were two very sad situations. I walked through my friend's divorce with him since we had known each other from his birth, lived in the same city, and, had been joined in relationship in the Body of Christ. What I did not know at the time, however, is that I would unexpectedly fall to the same fate.

Without going into details, in the spring of 1991 my wife decided she could do better with someone else, so, in the spring of 1992, she physically left me and our home. Like my friend and my brother, my wife left me for no Biblical reason. I had not committed adultery.

Although being separated and divorced we raised are two boys jointly. If a couple were to divorce, and I hate divorce, we would be the example to follow. We did all we could for the benefit of our sons. We are friends.

It took a lot of heart-felt fellowship with my brothers in Christ, especially Jim, and with Jesus to get me through that divorce. Many miracles took place during that time, far too many to tell you here. You can learn about some of these miracles and what the Bible really teaches about divorce and remarriage after divorce in my book entitled "Divorce, Remarriage, And God's Original Intention." There is much misunderstanding concerning what the Bible teaches on this issue. I believe, as others believe as well, I set forth the Biblical stance on this issue in a format we can all understand.

In past days of Evangelical Christianity, divorce was next to the unforgivable sin. Maybe in the eyes of some, it was actually the unforgivable sin. Those experiencing such a disaster in their lives were set on the side-lines of church activity. They were often seen as second-class Christians. They could come to a church meeting, give their financial donation, but that was it. Just sit in your pew and be quiet, was often the mentality.

The ostracizing of divorced and remarried Christians is not necessarily the case any more. There are so many divorced and remarried Christians these days that the church can no longer afford to sit these folk on the sideline. Someone needs to do the work necessary to keep church alive, and those once on the side-lines have been called back onto the field of church ministry.

I welcome this change, but, this change has come by way of a concession. By that I mean there are so many divorced people in any given congregation, they can no longer be ignored. Change should never come by way of a concession. Change should come from a proper, hermeneutical, understanding of what the Bible teaches, which again, I have set forth in my book entitled, "Divorce, Remarriage, And God's Original Intention." Okay, you're right. I'm doing a bit of advertising here.

One thing Jesus clearly and explicitly told me during the sad days of a marriage failure was that if I would live my life within the boundary of Scripture, He would look after me. He has certainly done that in miraculous form. Again, there are far too many miraculous interventions of the Lord on my behalf that took place in those days to inform you about in this little book.

Don't let anyone ever tell you that miracles ended with the first generation church, as some teach. That is a heresy, as they say, straight from the pit of hell. If you walk with Jesus, He will walk with you through the good times of life and through the sad times of life. Be assured, there will be sad times in life. As the old country song puts it: "I never promised you a rose garden." Jesus never promised us a life of ease. In fact look at what He told His disciples in John 16:33.

> "I have told you these things, so that in me you may have peace. In this world you will have trouble. But take heart! I have overcome the world."

No one suffers through a divorce without struggle, sadness, depression, frustration, pain, and turmoil, and that included me. That being said, there was always, and I do mean always, a great measure of underlying peace beneath all of the anguish that accompanied my marriage falling apart.

19
Get Lost

For most of my life I have been actively involved in church. I feel best about my life when I am serving Jesus in the context of the Body of Christ. I am not a pew sitter. I am not an "attend-a-meeting-only believer. I have done almost everything there is to do in church. I've dusted pews to preparing the yearly paperwork the government requires churches to do. What I enjoy most, though, is playing music on a worship team and teaching the Bible.

A new church began to be formed in Belleville in 1991 as a result of our church closing a couple years prior. I have mentioned that closure earlier. I became part of the church in the spring of 1992. As in previous years I found myself quite involved in church activities. As I just said, I am most happy in a church situation when I am functioning, actually doing something, that I feel called to do. It is what church is all about, and, it certainly is what I am all about.

My responsibilities within Belleville Community Church, as it was called, included such things as playing guitar, banjo, and harmonica, or "mouth organ" as my dad used to call it, on the worship team. I also had the opportunity to preach and teach the Bible, along with performing some administrative tasks for our pastor, all of which I enjoyed.

This church lasted about eleven years and sadly, it folded for a couple of reasons. Far too often Christians seem to be in the church building business, and I do not use the word "business" without giving it any thought. In much of the western-world, we build our sacred organizations as if they are a Fortune Five Hundred Corporation, while the concept of church being the Body of Christ gets ignored. I do understand the legalities and corporate structure of a modern-day, western-world church, but that should never take the place of the basic Biblical meaning to church. Well, this church-building business failed, and it failed, at least in my opinion, in a sad and unnecessary way.

Churches often fail because those in the church fail to understand that as individual believers, they have been called alongside of those to whom Jesus has placed them in church. We are called alongside of others in the Body of Christ, not just for support, but also to function in ministry together. When we fail to function in ministry in one unified body, we fail to represent Jesus to our surrounding culture as we were meant to do. It is for this reason that the church in our western world, in my thinking, has failed more often than not to succeed in its God-given mission.

About half way through this church's existence, our pastor arbitrarily, submitted our church under the authority of a man considered to be an apostle. I use the word "arbitrarily" because, as a group of people, we had no choice in the matter. Submitting our church to this apostle, and some questioned that he was an apostle, was our pastor's decision alone.

Just before this church disintegrated into a heap of dust, I was told by our pastor, and really, he was my friend, that because I did not embrace all of our apostle's teaching, I should think about moving to another church group. I found that difficult to hear. I could not believe, my friend and pastor, was encouraging me to move on. He asked me why I was a part of the church. I did not hesitate to answer. I told him that I was called alongside of real, living, born again, believers, to function with them in the service of the Lord.

According to my friend and pastor, that was not the reason why I should be a part of this church. What I needed to do was to fully embrace all of what our so-called apostle taught, and that I could not honestly do.

I do not believe that my brothers and sisters in Jesus have to hold to every Biblical position I embrace. For that reason, I can have fellowship with other Christians who may think differently than me on secondary Biblical issues. I believe the reverse should be true as well, but it was not so in this case. It was either "believe as I believe," or to put it bluntly, "get lost." Well, I was pretty much forced to leave, but I certainly did not get lost.

20
I'm From Eastern Canada

In March of 1994, I attended one of our usual Tuesday evening church Bible studies. Before the meeting began I made what I thought was an all-important, but light-hearted, announcement to our group that consisted of many single men and women. I repeated what I had heard on the daily news program that morning, which was this. Men living in Eastern Canada have a much easier time finding a wife than men living in Western Canada. That hit home to me because, I was now a single man, and, I lived in Eastern Canada. I figured this bit of news might find a place in the hearts and minds of those in the room that night.

As I said, there were a number of single men and women at the Bible study; so, I thought we would all get a bit of a chuckle about this vitally significant news flash, and that we did. We were all well informed, encouraged, and amused, as I walked back to my seat.

Just by chance, or should I say, a pre-arranged happenstance by God Himself, an attractive, new lady of my age, was visiting our Bible study that evening. She just happened to sit right in front of me. I mean I could reach out and touch her if I was so inclined, but of course, I was not so inclined, at least not at that precise moment. Touching would have to wait for another day. How impactful and significant this pre-arranged by the Lord, seating arrangement turned out to be.

Our pastor noticed this new addition to our study group so he asked her to stand and introduce herself, and so she did. She stood to her feet and said: "I am Dianne Bradley." Then, she turned around, looked directly at me, and without any hesitation said: "and I'm from Eastern Canada."

I was, for once in my life, speechless; just utterly dumbfounded. What could I possibly say in response? After hearing the importance of men finding wives in Eastern Canada earlier that day on the news program, this introduction was mind blowing. Here I am, a single man, living in Eastern Canada, and a single woman from Eastern Canada was actually sitting right in front of me. She was less than two feet away. Why did she turn around and specifically and intentionally address me as she did? Could this be some kind of divine intervention in my life? All that came to mind to speak in return was: "O no, what does that mean?"

A mutual friend had invited this new addition from Eastern Canada to our Bible study. I had never met Dianne before, and the first meeting was memorable, and, it certainly would not be the last meeting.

Now I admit this. Knowing that an attractive, middle-aged, lady, who by the way, was born and raised in Eastern Canada, was sitting a couple of feet in front of me, made if difficult to pay attention to the Bible study. How could I keep my mind on the Bible when the lady from Eastern Canada disabled my ability to think with any kind of intelligence?

Our mutual friend was going to drive Dianne home and would, just so happen, be driving by my street on the way, so guess what? I was asked if I would like a ride home as well. Little did I know that the new addition to our Bible study just lived two blocks from my house. I mean, I could walk to her house in a brief few minutes.

I would have normally walked home, but knowing that the lady from Eastern Canada would be in the car, what real choice did I have in the matter. I had no choice. It was a simple, completely logical, albeit, emotionally influenced, choice to make. I would accept the ride home without any hesitation, and that I did, but, not without a little embarrassing incident.

Upon entering the darkened parking lot from the bright lights of inside the building, I did something embarrassingly stupid. I still shake my head at this. I made the right hand turn into the parking lot a bit too soon and bang; I collided face first, with a cement wall. Can you believe that? Well, I couldn't. I was just a foot away from the lady from Eastern Canada and I had to go and bump into a wall. What an embarrassing example of a first impression.

Was I nervous? Was I pre-occupied? Was I just not thinking straight? Whatever the reason for the collision, that wall stopped me dead in my tracks.

Somewhat startled and surprised, Dianne turned around and looked at me. "Are you blind or something?" she asked. I answered in a matter-of-fact, but humorous way. "In fact, I am legally blind." Now, she was the one embarrassed for a fleeting few seconds, but because of my light-hearted response, her embarrassment subsided quickly. We both had a good laugh over that one.

I enjoyed the short trip home, but I did not get a lot of sleep that night. The lady from Eastern Canada occupied both my mind and my dreams.

After a couple of weeks had passed I got up the nerve to ask Dianne out for coffee. Two days before that coffee date, in a prayer meeting, another lady friend prophesied over me. She, by the inspiration of the Holy Spirit, predicted that my life would come into a new alignment. She had no idea that I had just asked Dianne out for coffee. She had no idea that I had feelings for Dianne. She knew nothing of these things. It was the Lord speaking through her to me. He can certainly do that.

I hope you realize that there are times that the Holy Spirit does speak through a person, and this was one of those times. Of course, not all who claim to speak by the Spirit of God are actually speaking by the Spirit of God. I know that to be true by both experience and by Scripture. If you read the apostle John's first letter you will see that he told us not to believe every spirit (1 John 4:1). Here is what John said.

> "Dear friends, do not believe every spirit, but test the spirits to see whether they are from God, because many false prophets have gone out into the world."

I had no problem believing this lady. I knew the lady who prophesied to me and I obviously knew the circumstances of my life that brought this prophecy home to my heart. This was yet another miracle of the Lord in my life that was attempting to recover from the devastation of divorce.

This too is a year-long story, but on May 13, 1995, Dianne Bradley, the lady from Eastern Canada, became Dianne Sweetman, my wife. My life was certainly brought into a new alignment, just as the prophetic word was told me. Jesus did look after me, as He said He would during the depressing days of my divorce. I lived my life within the boundary of Scripture, as He mandated me. I did not head off to a local bar, seeking some comfort from some attractive lonely lady waiting for some attention from a lonely guy.

It's not rocket science. If you want Jesus to co-operate with you, you have to co-operate with Him. That shouldn't be all that difficult to figure out.

Me, 1994, when Dianne first met me

Our wedding - May 13 - 1995

21
Good-bye Bill

In and around 1998, Dianne's brother Bill was dying from cancer in a Hamilton, Ontario, hospital. He was all alone. He had no wife. His brother died decades earlier. His parents were not in the best health and lived too far away to visit him. He was only in his late forties. There was just Dianne, his sister. Hamilton is a three plus hour drive west from Belleville, and that depended on how busy the traffic was around Toronto.

It was a Saturday evening when we were visiting Bill. We were told that he just had a week or two to live, and, maybe even just days. It was about eight thirty in the evening when I told Bill that we had a three hour drive ahead of us and so we had to leave him and go home. That was tough on us, but we felt we had little choice. Both Dianne and I really felt bad about leaving Bill to die alone, and it turned out that he did not have to die all by himself. This turned out to be one of the most awesome miracles that I have ever, in my entire life, been involved in.

I told Bill that I would pray that Jesus would take him. I meant, take him right then and now, not tomorrow, not next week, but right now. Bill was too far gone to talk, but Dianne and I were convinced he could hear us. I encouraged Bill to tell Jesus that he was ready to leave this world and that he wanted to be with Him, as of right now. I, then, laid my hand on Bill, and in a short three to five second prayer I asked Jesus to take Bill. That was it. It was not a heavy-duty, spiritual-sounding, prayer. I have never, in my entire life, had a prayer of mine answered so quickly. Immediately, as in the next five seconds, after I asked Jesus to take Bill, He breathed two deep breaths, and then he passed into eternity. He was gone. He was with Jesus in Heaven.

To assist someone passing from this life into the next life with Jesus, as Dianne and I did that Saturday evening, is beyond words of explanation. Yes, in one sense of the word, it was a sad moment, but still, no English words can really convey that moment. It was more than awesome, more than incredible, and more than any other word that you can come up with. It was a miracle.

After Bill left us, Dianne told me that he had one lonely tear slide down his cheek as I was praying for him. I knew he heard my prayer. I also knew Jesus heard my prayer. Bill was certainly ready to make his transition from this life into the next life. What a miracle.

22
Figuring Out Church.

Personally speaking, I do not believe in shopping for a church, or, trying a church out for size, as I have heard some call it. Far too often, in our western-world church, Christians move from one church group to another with great ease. They look for the style of worship music they like. They look for what they would call a good preacher. They want a youth group that supports their needs. There are as many reasons why people want to settle into a particular church as there are people looking for that church.

It is my thinking that there is one reason for our placement in church. We should not be looking for that which benefits us but, we should be asking ourselves this question. To whom is Jesus placing me alongside in the Body of Christ where I can develop personal relationships in order for me to function in my calling as a servant of the Lord. Church is more than a place that meets our needs. It's a place where the individual is to serve in ministry with those to whom they have been called alongside. It is the lack of this mentality that has weakened the effectiveness of the western-world church in our individualistic, unbiblical, secular culture.

Nevertheless, for the next three years after our church folded in the spring of 2002, Dianne and I went on a search for a new church home. Both Dianne and I were used to being involved in church, so, it was only natural for me, and for Dianne as well, to find a new church home. I am not saying we went about this the right way, but off we went. We attended Sunday morning meetings of three different church groups over the next three year period, all of which, didn't seem to work for us. Maybe we just were not listening to the Lord as we should have.

As I have said above, for me, church is all about being properly joined to others in both supportive relationships and ministry in the local expression of the Body of Christ, otherwise known as the church. If church was all about sitting in a pew for an hour or two every Sunday morning, I would rather sit at home on my deck, drinking a hot cup of coffee, and that is what we ended up doing for nine years, after we failed to find a new church family over the previous three years.

Since I had been leading a home Bible study at the time, Dianne and I were invited to join the home-group leaders team in the first church we attended. I thought this would be a great way to enter into ministry among these people, but, these people were far from friendly. I will not go into the details but because of a lack of friendliness, we moved onto another church group. I tell you this. The lack of friendly people in a church group is devastating for the growth, and the good health, of that church.

We had friends in the next church group, as we did in the first group. I have friends in many church groups. I actually got to play my guitars on one of the worship teams in our second attempt at church, but once again, things did not work out for various reasons, so again, we moved on. Believe it or not, the pastor's wife in this second group was so unfriendly that she failed to acknowledge my presence when I would say "hi" to her from two feet away. She would simply walk away as if she never saw me, but of course, she did see me. She was not blind. Allow me to suggest, that is not Christian love.

The third and last church we visited on our mission to find a new church home was being split in half when we first began to attend Sunday meetings. That was sure a comforting introduction to a new church setting. Of course, it was not comforting.

I was being asked by people on both sides of the dispute to become a voting member of the church. There was only one reason for this, and that was so I could vote to either kick the pastor out or keep him in his position. I would not become an official member of a church just so I could vote. Official membership, in my opinion, is Biblically questionable anyway. Such a political style referendum is not New Testament thinking.

It was a sad Sunday morning when the result of the vote was announced. The pastor, who has since become a close friend of mine, lost his position by a fraction of a percentage point of the vote. One man who was on the losing side of the vote got up from his pew and stomped out of the sanctuary in anger. As he walked out of that Sunday gathering of the saints, we all heard him yell out: "Enjoy the fire and brimstone you bastards." Remember, this was a meeting of the saints. For me, the whole situation was no different than a political election one would experience in the United States, or here in Canada. That did it for me concerning the traditional church, and that is why, for the next nine years, I, and my wife, Dianne spent Sunday mornings at home.

Let it be known, for me, even though I was not a part of a traditional church, I was still a part of the Body of Christ. I did not disassociate myself from those brothers in the Lord to whom Jesus had joined me over the years. I was still in fellowship, as the New Testament defines fellowship.

The Greek word "koinonia" is translated into English as "fellowship` in our English New Testament. This word, in its New Testament context, means much more than sharing a conversation over a cup of coffee, as we might think these days. Koinonia, or fellowship, in Biblical terms is the sharing of your life with those to whom Jesus has placed you alongside in the Body of Christ. This is a New Testament concept that is not always seen or experienced in our western-world church.

If attending meetings are important to you, I did attend meetings of believers. I actually led a home Bible study group during those nine years. Our study group lasted for sixteen years, before we had to shut it down because of illness on the part of the couple whose house we had gathered for our Bible study.

23
Home Bible Study

In the summer of 2002 I was asked by some of my brothers and sisters in the Lord to start and then lead, a home Bible study group. I was somewhat reluctant to take on this challenge at first, but thinking it over, I decided to go forward and perform the task at hand and help people understand the Bible better.

Before taking on this challenge, I made everyone aware that we would study the book of Romans, one of my favourite books of the Bible. We would delve into the book verse by verse, and at times, word by word. This would be a detailed study of Paul's letter to the Romans, which among other things, sets forth the basic teachings of the Christian faith. More than any other Biblical author, it was Paul who set forth the theology of salvation. If Paul got things wrong, then we as Christians are in one big mess.

I made it clear from the very beginning that when we finished our study of Romans, I would ask the people if they would like to continue onto another book of the Bible.

Our study of Romans took more than a year, and when it was all said and done, I asked everyone if they would like to continue. Without any hesitation, they all said "yes," and so we continued for sixteen years, until the day came when we decided to close things down because of health concerns of the couple in whose house we had gathered for all of those years.

To make it clear, we stopped meeting together on a regular basis because of health conditions, not because of any theological dispute or relational issues. We did not shut down our relationships. Church is first and foremost about properly relating to Jesus and those to whom He has placed us in His present-day body. Church is much more than meetings.

One of the important outcomes for me concerning this Bible study group was that as I prepared for the weekly study, I wrote a commentary on what we would study and then I posted it on my web site, which you can find at: www.stevesweetman.com. I admit, the farther we went on in our study, the better and more informative my commentaries became.

Writing these commentaries has been a major undertaking for me. I have spent thousands of hours since 2002 putting these Bible commentaries together. The most detailed and I would say, the most instructive of my commentary projects, can now be found on most all Amazon platforms. It is called "An Elderly Man Speaks," my commentary on 1 John. The compilation of that commentary took me at least four hundred and fifty hours to work through, and a couple of more hundred hours for my friend Tim, as he helped me with the spelling, grammar, and theological issues. It is a three hundred and ninety one page, exegetical, verse by verse commentary. It is based on sound Biblical interpretation, called hermeneutics. My comments are also based on the letter's cultural setting and Greek grammar and definitions of words. For your information, if you do not already know, the New Testament was written in first-century common, every-day Greek. The more knowledge one has concerning New Testament style Greek grammar and definition of words, along with knowledge of first-century, Greco-Roman, culture, the better chance one will have in understanding what the New Testament teaches.

24
www.stevesweetman.com

It was in the year 2000 that I created a web site for my brother's wedding service in Niagara Falls, Ontario, Canada. Since I discovered how to actually do such a thing, I decided I would make a web site for myself, and that I did. I called it "About Jesus." As of 2019, it is still in existence and can be found at www.stevesweetman.com.

My web site has been a form of ministry for me over the years. I do not even have to leave the house to have some kind of impact on the lives of those who might visit my site and benefit from it. I bet you that the apostle Paul would have loved to have his own web site, and probably Facebook and Twitter as well. How many more letters we would have today if Paul could have simply shot off an email instead of dictating a letter to be written for him. I wonder how many Facebook friends Paul would have had, if there had have been such a thing in his day.

In and around 2009 my web site took a boost in popularity. My name and email address had been on the subscriber list of a prominent American Bible teacher. For some reason he was having computer server problems and was sending out blank emails to thousands of people around the world who had signed up to receive his email reports. With so many of these blank emails finding their way into my inbox, I decided to send one back, but, with one of my articles in it. Bingo, it happened. To my surprise, and for some reason, this ministry's computer server sent my article out to thousands of people around the world. My web site had a few thousand hits over the next couple of days. As a result, many people around the globe asked me to add them to my email list.

From my email list, every Monday I send an article to people in Canada, the United States, Guatemala, New Zealand, England, Germany, India, Vietnam, parts of Africa, and probably some countries I have missed in my list. Beyond that, I don't know who forwards my articles to others and where they end up. I do know that some people pass my articles onto others. One man, before he died, forwarded my articles to about nine hundred people on his email list. Isn't email great.

One Christian pastor in California emailed me after my article was sent to him from this prominent Bible teacher's computer server. He was quite upset with me because he thought I had hacked into this American Bible teacher's, who was his friend, web site and was the cause of all these spam emails. I assured him that was not the case. I am not that internet literate to do such a thing, even if I wanted to do it. Of course, I would never want to do such a thing. When he checked out my web site, and saw, in his words, "that I was just an ordinary person, without a full-fledged ministry, which included a board of directors and legal status," his anger subsided.

The whole dialogue with this upset pastor from California just re-enforced in my mind that there are so many Christians out there that do not understand Christian ministry. Any brief reading of 1 Corinthians 14 should make it clear that every Christian, none excluded, is called to be some kind of minister of the gospel. There is no special clergy, set aside to be an elite Christian. I guess he figured an ordinary guy like me would be no threat to his friend's ministry.

Over the years, and beyond my web site, I have extended my online Bible teaching ministry to both Facebook and YouTube. YouTube has become a place where many people have listened to my Bible teaching, and that again, by a bit of an accidental miracle. Is there such a thing as an accidental miracle? Probably not. It just sounded good so I typed it into this paragraph.

Crowder is my favourite Christian band. I posted one of their songs on my YouTube channel for one reason only. I needed some kind of format to play one of their songs during a Sunday sermon I preached. That was the easiest way for me to get the song, with its lyrics on the church's overhead screen and the music on the church's sound system.

Little did I know that Crowder's song, that was meant for one congregation only, would get around two million people listening to it, to date. Many of those who listened to that song have requested to be on my YouTube subscription list. Prior to adding that song to my YouTube channel, I had a grand total of three subscribers. Yes, three whole subscribers. I now have more than three thousand two hundred people who subscribe to all that I post on my YouTube channel, and there are lots to discover there. The list of subscribers keeps growing on a daily basis. Once again, this form of ministry goes around the world, and, I do not even have to leave my computer chair to teach the Bible. Technology is amazing. I choose to use it in the service of the Lord.

25
Ordained To Ministry

It was during August 2015, when on more than one occasion I believe I heard Jesus telling me that come 2016 there would be a change in my and Dianne's life. The change concerned church. What that meant, I had no clue.

As I mentioned earlier, for nine years Dianne and I had not been a part of what I call a "traditional church." I was, however, still a member of the Body of Christ. To remove myself from the Body of Christ would be to remove myself from Christ Jesus, and that I would never do.

What Jesus meant when He told me that things would change when it came to church, was unknown to me at the time, but, in a couple of months, the plan was beginning to be unfolded before my legally blind eyes.

Dianne and I walked out our front door to take our little Bichon dog named Jesse for a walk. It was in October, 2015, about a month and a half after hearing from the Lord about this upcoming change in our lives. Within the first minute of our walk we met a lady, namely Safron, who I had played music with on our church's worship team in the 1990's. She had just left her car at a local garage to get repaired. She, just one minute earlier, asked Jesus to help her meet someone on her walk home, and there we were. Another very quick answer to a short little prayer. Sometimes prayers get, I would say, answered unexpectedly fast. That was certainly one of those prayers.

Safron explained to us all about her church situation and that her and another mutual friend, that being Heather, were leading one of three worship teams in a local congregation. She sounded quite excited about it. Before she left us on her walk home, she casually suggested that her, Heather, and Heather's husband Troy, get together with us for dinner sometime. That took place the next month in November, 2015.

We had a great time of fellowship and reminiscing over dinner. While we were ending our meal I discovered the real reason for our get-together. It was not to talk about the good-old days as I thought, although that we did.

Safron turned to Heather and asked. "Should we ask him now?"

Now in suspense, I asked myself: "What does that mean?" Obviously, there was an ulterior motive for this meal.

Heather responded and said: "Sure, go ahead and ask him."

"Would you like to be a part of our worship team?" Safron asked.

Both girls, ladies, or whatever you call women in their late forties, knew how I felt about the traditional church, so, they said that I would not have to attend every Sunday meeting. I would only have to attend the Sunday meetings that our team would be leading in worship.

Well, my heart sank to my stomach when I heard their request. I did not want to become a member of another traditional style church, but, I have always had a difficult time saying no to these women. They are my good friends. I answered them by saying that the next time they led worship, Dianne and I would be there. I would see how I felt then.

I also told them that if I was ever to join their worship team, I could not just attend the particular Sunday meeting we were leading worship. Church for me was full involvement, not just playing music every three weeks.

To make yet another long story way too short, through a number of miracles, I was on their worship team. Since then I have played my electric Fender guitar, my Martin guitar, my Yamaha classical guitar, my banjo, my mandolin, and my harmonicas.

It is ironic, that soon after Jesus told me that when it came to church, things would change for Dianne and I, things began to change, and, I came close to closing the door on the change. How sad for Dianne and I if I had have closed that door. It tells me this. We really do need to have an ear open to the inner voice of the Holy Spirit. We should be in tune enough with Jesus that we recognize the importance, or, lack of importance, of all things that come our way. We need to pay attention to what He might say to us, and, if you are a true Christian, He will speak to you.

This change of church has been one of the best blessings from Jesus in years for me. I am totally involved, not just in music, but, in teaching the Bible, and leadership within this, what I call, a semi-traditional church. That suits me just fine.

I was not seeking what I am about to tell you next. Our pastor, Trevor, suggested that I become an ordained minister. I've never really put a lot of stock or importance on becoming ordained, but I agreed to be an officially ordained minister of the gospel. On February 17, 2019, I was ordained through the Fellowship of Christian Assemblies (Canada - U.S.A.). My pastor and now friend, Trevor, told me that it was all about the recognition of the ministry that had already been well established in my life.

I am totally blown away, as the saying goes, to how accepted and loved I am in that congregation of believers. I have thanked Jesus over and over for this change in church that He has brought into my life. Once again, there were far too many miracles that took place along the way that got me to what is called Harvest Ministries. We gather, and minister, in our own building, which was once the city of Belleville's library. Prior to that, when it was built in the mid 1800's, it was a bank. I find it all interesting that a bank becomes a base for me to help invest the Word of the Lord into the lives of people. A library which is a place of study becomes a place where I can help to educate others in Biblical truth.

26
Cancer

One always thinks that cancer will strike someone else, but probably not one's self. That was my thinking when I was sitting in the doctor's office the last week of November, 2018. Just because I had a high PSA score on my PSA blood test did not mean I had prostate cancer. The odds were on my side, or so I thought. That thought process changed within two minutes of sitting before the doctor. I learned that in fact, like my dad, cancer had penetrated my prostate.

Hearing that one has been infected with cancer can be unsettling or even scary. I took the news in stride, or should I say, I took the news in the presence of the Lord. I experienced the inner peace that comes from knowing Jesus from the beginning to the end of the whole ordeal.

Within six weeks of hearing the news, on January 9, 2019, the surgeon removed my prostate. As I type these words in the autumn of 2019, I am in the process of recovering from my surgery, but most of all, I am free of cancer.

If the fact that I had prostate cancer was a test of faith from the Lord, and I'm not saying it was, I passed the test. I have trusted Jesus with all things in my life, and this cancer was no different than the rest of the things I have trusted Him for throughout my life.

Just in case you don't realize it, God can and will test the validity of your faith at times. Look at what the apostle Peter wrote in 1 Peter 1:6 and 7.

> "In all this you greatly rejoice, though now for a little while you may have had to suffer grief in all kinds of trials. These have come so that the proven genuineness of your faith — of greater worth than gold, which perishes even though refined by fire — may result in praise, glory and honor when Jesus Christ is revealed."

Those to whom Peter was writing were suffering from severe persecution. Some of them had been executed because of their association with Jesus. They were indeed suffering. Peter called this suffering a test of their faith.

Be assured. If you claim to possess genuine faith, your genuine faith will be tested. If you never have these tests, it might suggest that you have no real faith in Jesus, because if you indeed did have real faith, your faith would be tested. It is simple Biblical logic.

27
December 4, 2019

As I type these words in September, 2019, I am not quite sixty eight years old, but on December 4, 2019, I will be, what I once considered old and outdated. Me, being sixty eight years of age is hard for me to get my head around. It seems like just yesterday that I was sixteen years old. One thing that proves about me, and that is, I still have a good memory. I do remember what it was like to be sixteen. I recall the first time I ever held hands with a girl. Man, what a feeling for a fifteen year old guy. In our culture today, I would be considered behind the times. It's a sad moral state that a fifteen year old guy today has pretty much done it all when it comes to girls.

I also recall my dad saying that his body may be seventy years old, but his mind thinks like a sixteen year old. I now realize the truthfulness of dad's statement.

This is a fact of life. I have more of my life behind me to remember and less of my life ahead of me to anticipate. Such a thought process causes one to reflect on the entirety of his life. It also causes one, and that includes me, to wonder what kind of legacy one, and that also includes me, will have after he departs from this world. It is for this reason that I write this short account of my life as a Christian. It also accounts for why I have written all of my other books as well. I want to leave some kind of tangible legacy; something that can be touched, in remembrance of my life.

This is my prayer for however many days or years I have ahead of me. I pray that Jesus will keep me in relatively good health, at least, until I am eighty years old, so I can be actively involved in serving Him in some worthwhile capacity. If He gives me more than the next twelve years, I would count that as a blessing. My father asked for seventy good years from the Lord. He got his seventy years, but, he did not make it to eighty, as I hope and pray that I will. Dad made it to seventy seven years. Now that I think about it, seventy seven is kind of a Biblical number that dad might have wondered about. I won't comment on Biblical numbers here. You can study all of that out for yourself.

If you have dedicated your life to Jesus, as I have, maybe you think as I think. I want to finish my life as a born-again-of-the-Spirit believer, doing as much as I can for my Lord and Saviour. I want to complete that which God has called me to do, and I want to finish strong, and that I will as I submit myself to Jesus and His will for my life.

28
After All These Years

I had considered a number of titles for this book, but none of them really grabbed my attention, that is, until I inserted one of my favourite country music C D's into our car's stereo system. If you are not a country music fan, as I am, you will probably have never heard of the singing group named Sawyer Brown.

While riding in the passenger seat of our car as my wife Dianne was driving us down highway 401, I heard my favourite Sawyer Brown song through the car stereo speakers. The song is entitled "All These Years." "That's it," I thought. "After All These Years," subtitled, "my life as a Christian," would be the title to my book.

It is far from an easy process to put your life with Jesus, and for me, that is most of sixty eight years so far, into a short, concise, story, as I have attempted to do. Lots more has transpired in my life over the years than what you have read in the previous pages. Hopefully and prayerfully, lots more will take place in my life beyond this point in time. That may have to come in a revised addition of this book, which is quite easy with these Amazon books.

I came to the Lord Jesus at an early age. I am still walking with Him through all of the good times and through all of the not so good times. I am still a Christian after all of these years. It isn't the one who starts the race that wins the victor's prize. It's the one who finishes the race that becomes the champion. I want to finish the race, and I want to finish the race with a winning attitude. I do not want to wimp out and just painfully and pathetically crawl across the finish line in defeat. I want to be one of the countless champions that will appear before the Lord Jesus Christ at some future date, and that I plan to be.

There are many reasons why people hand their lives over to Jesus. For me, I did not submit myself to the rule of Jesus for just the benefits He offered me, and there have been many. I have handed my life over to Jesus because I have found Him to be the ultimate, universal truth. Once understanding that, I had no other logical choice to make but to submit my life over to Him.

My hope and prayer is for all who read my story, will find, like me, that the Lord Jesus Christ is indeed the ultimate, universal truth of all things spiritual and all things material. If you make this logical choice for your life, you will never regret it. You will find yourself among the myriad of people who will some day stand before the throne of God and the Lord Jesus Christ, as pictured here in Revelation 7:9 and 10.

> "After this I [John] looked, and there before me was a great multitude that no one could count, from every nation, tribe, people and language, standing before the throne and before the Lamb. They were wearing white robes and were holding palm branches in their hands. And they cried out in a loud voice: 'Salvation belongs to our God, who sits on the throne, and to the Lamb.'"

My heart's desire and prayer is that I will see all of you in this great multitude of people. Together, we will stand before the throne of God, worshipping God our Father and the Lord Jesus Christ, our Saviour. We will have received God's grace, that is, His undeserved favour in our lives, and, His divine ability to do and to be that which He desires. We will have made it to the victorious end of this present age as a champion. Words cannot convey, neither can our minds conceive, the majestic and ecstatic worship experience that will envelop us on that day.

I hope to see you there.

29

The Process Of Salvation

Many people may think that salvation, or as we often say, getting saved, is a one time, instantaneous experience. In one sense of the word it is that. There does come a point in time when one steps up to the line of salvation, so to speak, and then crosses over the line and is saved. On the other hand, there is a process that takes place prior to crossing that line, and really, even after crossing that line.

The New Testament speaks of salvation in three verb tenses. I was saved. I am being saved, and, I will be saved.

I was saved. Romans 8:24 reads:

> "For in this hope we were saved. But hope that is seen is no hope at all. Who hopes for what they already have?"

I am being saved. 2 Corinthians 2:15 reads:

> "For we are to God the pleasing aroma of Christ among those who are being saved and those who are perishing."

I will be saved. Romans 5:10 reads:

> "For if, while we were God's enemies, we were reconciled to him through the death of his Son, how much more, having been reconciled, shall we be saved through his life!"

All this means that at one point in my life I got saved. During my life as a Christian, salvation is being worked out in my daily life, until the day comes when Jesus returns to earth. On that day I will be completely saved because Jesus will transform who I am into being like who He presently is. 1 John 3:2 says it this way.

> "Dear friends, now we are children of God, and what we will be has not yet been made known. But we know that when Christ appears, we shall be like him, for we shall see him as he is."

The beginning step of salvation is when you first hear the message of salvation. You may not fully understand the message, and you may even ignore it before you choose to accept it or reject it.

Prior to making your decision, whether for or against the message of salvation, the Holy

Spirit will speak to your heart. As a matter of fact, you cannot come to Jesus and accept His message of salvation unless God the Father, through His Spirit, draws you to Jesus and helps you understand the message of salvation you hear. John 6:44 puts it this way.

> "No one can come to me unless the Father who sent me draws them, and I will raise them up at the last day."

The gospel message that you hear is that you, at the very core of who you are, consistently misses the mark of God's righteous requirements for your life. This is called your sinful human nature that all human beings possess from conception. It will eventually lead you to what the Bible calls the "Lake of Fire" (Revelation 20:15). Jeremiah 17:9 in the Christian Standard Bible describes this sinful nature. That verse reads:

> "The heart is deceitful above all things and beyond cure. Who can understand it?"

The first step in the process of salvation is, thus, admitting that you are more sinful than you realize and that with God's help, you want to walk away from living life on your own terms. The Bible calls this repentance.

Once understanding this, the message you hear tells you to hand your life over to Jesus so He can direct all of the affairs of your life. The Bible calls this faith. Faith is simply trust, as in, I now trust my life with Jesus.

It is vital to understand that faith, or, believing in Jesus, is more than believing in His existence in your mind. The devil and his demons believe in the existence of God and they fear for their lives according to James 2:19. Since Biblical believing means trust, faith in Jesus means you have come to trust your life with Him.

Once you, by the help of the Holy Spirit, agree with God that you are sinful at the core of who you are, and, once you submit, or trust, your life to Jesus, you, at some point will receive His Spirit into your life and you will be saved. This may take some time, or it may not take any time at all, but once the Holy Spirit comes into your life, your life will begin to change into that which Jesus wants it to be.

The reception of the Holy Spirit into your very being is the proof, or God's legal seal, that you have been saved. Ephesians 1:13 reads:

> "And you also were included in Christ when you heard the message

of truth, the gospel of your salvation. When you believed, you were marked in him with a seal, the promised Holy Spirit ..."

Once you receive the Holy Spirit into your life, you have stepped onto the path of salvation that leads to your ultimate salvation when you meet Jesus face to face.

In conclusion, the process of salvation is admitting that you are separated from God and that you are more sinful than what you realize. This is called repenting. Once repenting, you hand your entire life over to Jesus so He can give you His Spirit. In Biblical terms, this is called faith, or believing. The Holy Spirit will then come into your very being. He will enable you to live for Jesus as you should. He will help you work out the life of salvation you have entered into. You, in fact will become a new creation, someone different than you have ever been. 2 Corinthians 5:17 confirms this.

"Therefore, if anyone is in Christ, the new creation has come: The old has gone, the new is here!"

Being a Christian is far more than adopting a Biblical belief system by which you live. It is receiving God's Spirit into your life that causes you to become someone you have never been.

About The Author

I live with my wife Dianne in Ontario, Canada where I was born in 1951. My entire life has been spent within what has been traditionally called Evangelical Christianity. I have read the Bible from an early age, but I have been a serious student of the Bible since 1970. I attended Elim Bible Institute and College in Lima, New York, U.S.A. in the mid 1970's. My passion in life is to not just study and teach the Bible but to allow its message to be lived out in my daily life and experience. Bible study is more than an intellectual pursuit for me. It is a life-changing endeavour that is producing the very life of Jesus my Lord and Saviour in my existence on this planet.

When it comes to church, I have done pretty much everything one can do as a layperson. From sweeping the floors, to preaching on a Sunday morning, and filling out yearly government forms - I have pretty much done it all. What I enjoy most is teaching the Bible and playing guitar, banjo, mandolin, and harmonica, as part of a worship team that loves to worship Jesus in song.

You can learn more about me and my teaching by visiting my web site at www.stevesweetman.com. It has been in existence since the year 2000. I add to it almost on a daily basis. You can also find me on YouTube and Facebook, both of which I use to share Biblical truth. I like to say that I am a Bible teacher with a prophetic edge. That simply means that hopefully my teaching is personally relevant in the daily lives of those to whom my teaching reaches.

On a personal note, I have been legally blind since birth. Bible study for me takes much effort. I read with one eye as my nose scrapes across the printed page, and I do so with the use of a magnifier in the right lens of my glasses. The tip of my nose often gets black from the ink on the printed page. As I type these words with the assistance of large-print software my nose is less than one inch from my twenty-seven-inch monitor, but that's okay. Jesus has blessed me beyond measure over the decades. Besides His biggest blessing of salvation, He healed me of Juvenile Diabetes at the age of six years old. I would not be alive today to type these words if not for the grace of our Lord Jesus Christ and His amazing power to heal sick bodies. The doctors at Sick Children's Hospital in Toronto, Ontario, Canada, called it a miracle. They just didn't attribute the miracle to Jesus. As a result of my deliverance from this devastating illness my father handed his life over to Jesus. Dad now resides in his heavenly home along with my mother.

I hope and pray that what you have read in this book will have been somewhat instructive and thought-provoking. I certainly do not claim to have all of the answers to all of our questions. I am still digging my way through the pages of the Bible to learn and understand all I can, as I hope you are doing as well.

In closing, I would like to thank you for both reading and purchasing my book.

Other books of mine you can purchase on many Amazon platforms include:

Divorce, Remarriage, and God's Original Intention

Will I Ever See My Buddy Again (God, pets, and eternity)

The Age of the Messiah (the thousand year rule of Christ on earth)

Living in the Light of Scripture - Volume 1, Volume 2, Volume 3, and Volume 4

Revisiting Pentecost (rethinking the Baptism

in the Holy Spirit)

Irrevocable Promises (the Abrahamic Covenant and Bible Prophecy)

The Politics of God and the Bible

Plurality Of Elders (the New Testament Pattern)

An Elderly Man Speaks (my commentary on 1 John)

You can contact me at:
www.stevesweetman.com
ssweetman11@cogeco.ca
sweetman1951@gmail.com
Face Book, under Steve Sweetman

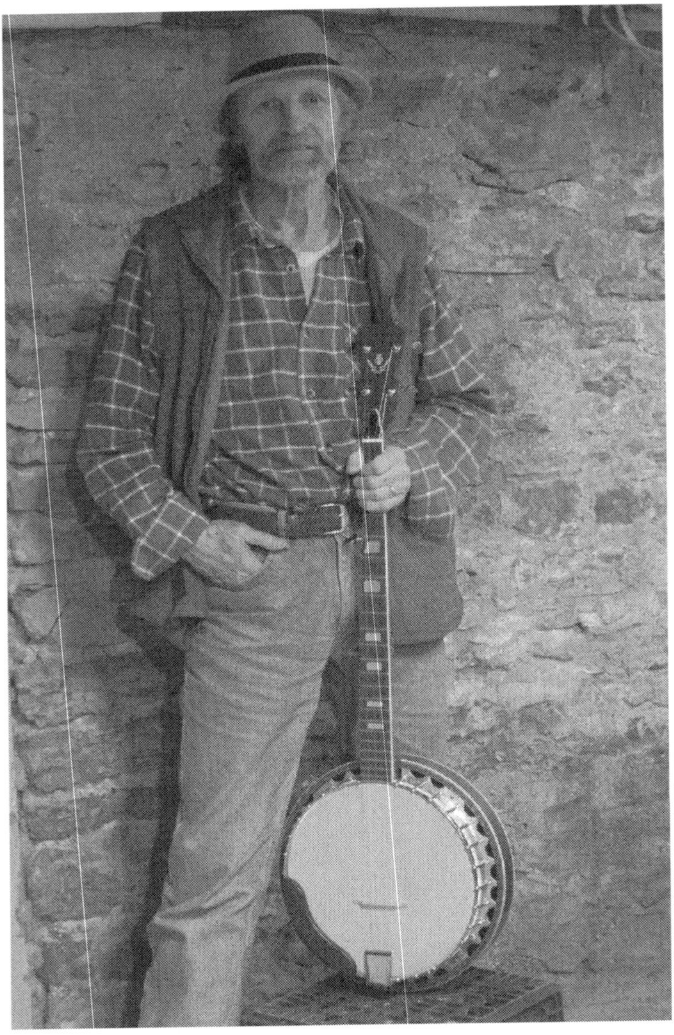

Made in the
USA
Monee, IL